ELTON JOHN

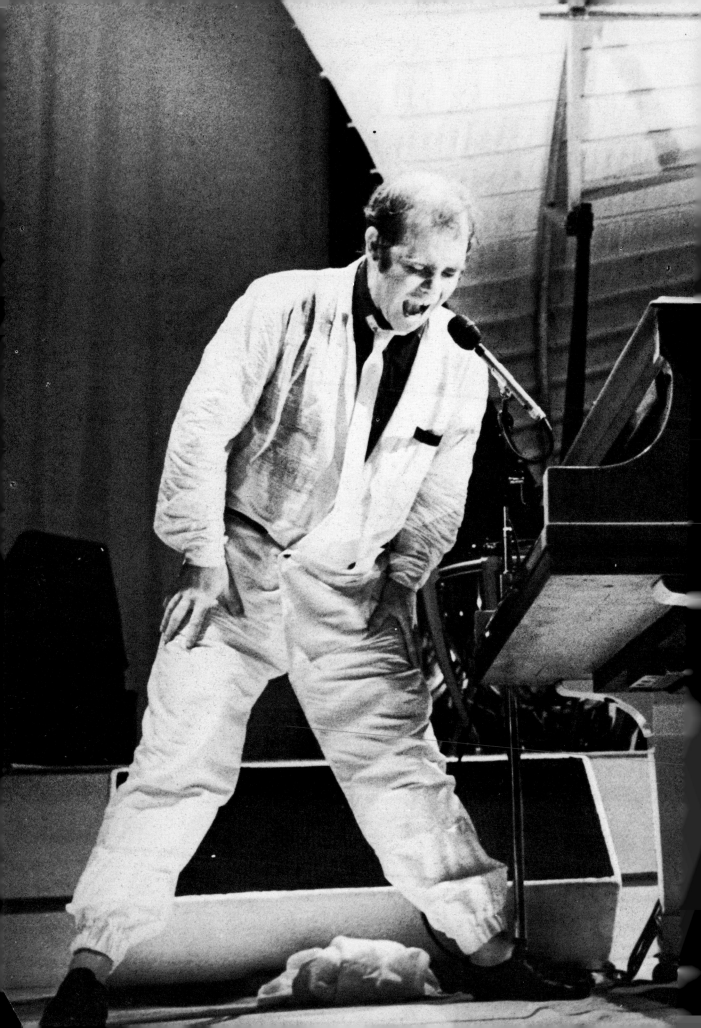

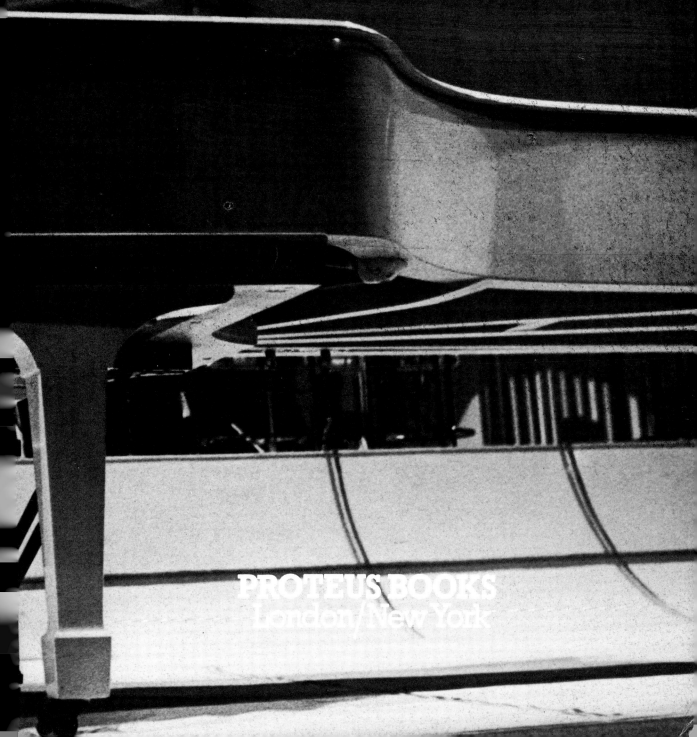

ELTON JOHN

BY PAUL ROLAND

PROTEUS BOOKS
London/New York

ACKNOWLEDGEMENTS

I acknowledge the following publications as sources of material and thank those who allowed me access to their archives: Sounds, Melody Maker, New Musical Express, Record Mirror, Zigzag, The Sun, News of the World, Sunday People, Daily Mirror, Daily Express, Daily Mail.

Thanks also to Tim Stewart for archive material and David Hancock for encouragement.

This book is dedicated to my Mother and Father, without whom . . .

PROTEUS BOOKS is an imprint of The Proteus Publishing Group

United States
PROTEUS PUBLISHING COMPANY, INC.
9, West 57th Street, Suite 4503
New York, NY 10019

distributed by:
CHERRY LANE BOOKS COMPANY, INC.
P.O. Box 430
Port Chester, NY 10573

United Kingdom
PROTEUS BOOKS LIMITED
Bremar House, Sale Place
London W2 1PT

ISBN 0 86276 201 4 (paperback)
ISBN 0 86276 202 2 (hardback)

First published in U.S. 1984
First published in U.K. 1984

Copyright © 1984 Proteus Books and Paul Roland

Photocredits: Alpha Press Agency, Aquarius Literary Agency, Ian Dickson, Keystone Press Agency, Barry Plummer, David Redfern, Retna, Rex Features, Ebet Roberts, Kay Rowley, Frank Spooner Pictures, Sport and General Press Agency, Star File.

Editor: Mike Teasdale

Designed by: Adrian J. Hodgkins
Typeset by: Type Generation
Printed in England by JB Offset, Marks Tey, Colchester, Essex

CONTENTS

FOREWORD

The roar that greeted the happy couple as they emerged from the tiny Anglican church of St. Mark's was quite deafening. The exclusive Sydney suburb of Darling Point had never seen anything quite like this.

Loudspeakers which only moments before had relayed the fifty minute service to the 2,000 strong crowd of Australian fans and well wishers went silent. The guests filed from the church to waiting limousines and luxurious private buses which sped them to a sumptious wedding breakfast at the nearby Sebel Town House Hotel.

The groom, resplendent in white silk morning coat, purple shirt, black trousers, and boater was none other than Elton John, multi-millionaire superstar of rock and chairman of Watford Football Club. His sudden and unexpected engagement to German born brunette Renata Blauel had captured the headlines of every major world newspaper. There were even complaints that some newspapers had virtually ignored the death of Soviet leader Yuri Andropov in their rush to cover Elton's marriage.

No one could doubt that this was the wedding of the year. As Renata, dressed in a white organdie silk and lace gown, swept into the hotel's spacious ballroom she was greeted by the sight of walls festooned with thousands of red and white roses,

Elton marries Renata Blauel on Valentine's Day in a small Sydney church; they then leave for a honeymoon in New Zealand and return to London six weeks later.

carnations and white orchids flown in specially from New Zealand. Elton had spared no expense for this Valentine's Day celebration to end them all. Wine and champagne were sent over from France. The assembled celebrities dined on pork, venison, truffles, lobster, quail, Queensland mud crab, mountain trout, Tasmanian scallops and tropical fruit. A six foot high floral centrepiece with the letters E&R adorned the head table and the £100,000 reception was topped off with a five-tier wedding cake.

Elton's manager John Reid was best man. Lyricist Bernie Taupin and his wife were also in attendance. Calls of congratulations came from Yoko Ono and from Elton's old friend Rod Stewart. Hollywood could scarcely have done better. In the midst of a resurgence in his popularity, Elton managed to attract the sort of attention usually reserved for royalty. His most recent album, *Too Low For Zero*, had been declared Elton's best-selling LP for a decade. He unveiled plans for an extensive tour, visiting twenty-one countries, including several behind the Iron Curtain. It was all very different from the lean years of the Sixties and his childhood in Pinner. . .

Elton John, rock's most unlikely superstar, was born Reginald Kenneth Dwight in Pinner, Middlesex on 25 March 1947. His mother Sheila aroused his interest in music at an early age. To keep him occupied she would sit him in front of an upright piano and allow him to bang away for hours. It wasn't long however until Reg taught himself to play by ear. He was soon developing a love of music which was encouraged by his mother who had a fairly large collection of 78's by Frankie Lane, Guy Mitchell, Johnny Ray and others and would let Reg stay up late to play for her friends at parties.

Stanley, his father, had been a professional trumpeter in the R.A.F. and had a rather cool attitude towards his progeny. Elton later admitted that he was frightened of his father whom he looked upon as somewhat of a snob. When Reg was nine his mother brought home two records that were to change his musical outlook — Bill Haley's *ABC Boogie* and Elvis Presley's *Heartbreak Hotel* — two seminal influences with lasting power. Like many of his generation it was after hearing these first rumblings of rock'n'roll that Reg Dwight made up his mind either to become a rock star or at least work in the music business.

He doggedly continued with his piano practise until at the age of twelve the offer of a music scholarship gave him the benefit of invaluable training. It entitled him to free lessons at the Royal Academy of Music in London on Saturday afternoons but infringed on his other passion, football. 'My father insisted I went, rather than play football', he remembers. 'He was in the R.A.F. and very strict. He wouldn't let me play football in the garden. I remember, sometimes, I used to skip lessons and just ride around on the Tube in London. I always used to hide away and play Jerry Lee Lewis records at 78 r.p.m. instead of at 45. Then I used to mime him. But I had a terrible inferiority complex.' His 'complex' was obviously based on his chubby appearance and all the insensitive jeering his schoolfriends would subject him too.

His natural gift for playing the piano became a refuge from the strict regime his father would impose. When the other children in the neighbourhood were allowed fashionable Fifties casual wear little Reg was packed off to school in baggy trousers and forbidden to kick a football around the garden for fear of damaging his father's rosebushes. Elton cites this oppressive atmosphere as a possible reason for his love of the outrageous, flamboyant, and expensive. But if his parents had not insisted on three hours piano practice a day would he have lacked the techinque to back up his natural ability?

As far as his academic career goes Elton felt he could have gone a lot further 'I never achieved what I could have done because I knew I wanted to do something else. I wanted to sing like Elvis.'

When he was thirteen his parents were divorced, though his mother later remarried. His new father, Fred Fairbrother, was a decorator by trade, and was far more encouraging towards his stepson's ambitions.

Reg joined his first group while he was still a schoolboy. He met Stuart Brown, a friend of his cousin who played guitar. 'I was very fat', Elton recalled, 'and when I said I played piano he laughed helplessly.' A quick demonstration of his Jerry Lee Lewis impersonation soon wiped the smile off Stuart's face and they formed a band, The Corvettes (after a brand of shaving cream). They played the usual run of scout huts without the aid of amplifiers (!) and fizzled out after a few months.

Around this time Reg became much enamoured with Buddy Holly and took to wearing black-rimmed specs in order to emulate his new hero. The problem was that after a year of wearing them he found he could not see without them. He had become shortsighted. 'I only needed them to see the blackboard and for reading. But I started becoming a Buddy Holly fan and began wearing them all the time to be like Holly. As a result, I soon became genuinely short-sighted.'

Two years after the schoolboy band he got himself a weekend job playing piano in a local pub. He was under age and had to be taken in by

INGERS

his mum and while she sat in a corner he pounded out Jim Reeves songs. It earned him a pound a night and he had soon saved up enough for an electric piano. The experience was later recalled in the track *Bitter Fingers* on the autobiographical *Captain Fantastic* album.

The electric piano came in very useful when he bumped into Stuart Brown again and they decided to have another try at forming a working band. At first there were four; Reg, Stuart, and Mick Inkpen and Rex Bishop from the first schoolboy group. They recruited a trumpeter and a tenor sax player through an advert in the music papers. The current wave of interest in R & B dictated the direction of the band and so Bluesology was formed. The name came from a Django Reinhardt record and the material inspired Reg to take the occasional vocal honours. But Steve Brown was not willing to let the spotlight wander from him and Reg grew increasingly frustrated at taking a backseat. Bluesology made two singles for Fontana, *Come Back Baby* on which Reg took lead vocal, and *Mr Frantic*. Both flopped and Reg's enthusiasm waned.

Still in the band he took up the offer of a job at Mills Music Publishers in Denmark Street in the West End of London and lived on £4.50 per week. The job consisted of parcelling sheet music, running errands and making tea and necessitated his leaving school early. His music teacher naturally objected but Reg felt this might be his only chance to enter the music business — it was a start anyhow.

A competition for local talent at the Kilburn State cinema led to an offer to back soul legend Wilson Pickett. Personalities didn't mix and in order to keep up the momentum Bluesology went all out to secure the job of backing Major Lance instead. They bought every one of the singer's records and learned them all note for note. Lance was impressed and they were hired. The U.K. tour was very successful and went a long way towards building the band's confidence but the touring commitments made it impossible for Reg to keep his job at Mills and he reluctantly left. Soul music loomed larger in his influences now and he admitted to being snobbish about it. At the same time the group underwent personnel changes which saw the departure of Mick, Rex, Pat and Dave and the arrival of six new members. Among them were brass player Elton Dean and guitarist Caleb Quaye.

In 1967 Bluesology were hired to back Long John Baldry on a U.K. tour, a tour Baldry still remembers with affection because Reg was taking pills to reduce his weight which also made him

Elton with Nigel Olsson (drums) and Dee Murray

short-tempered. 'He shouted a lot which I found amusing' said LJB.

It was during this constant touring that Reg fell in love with a girl called Linda and for six months he was enamoured with her but she tormented him with constant pleas to quit the music business and settle down. Eventually she drove him to a suicide attempt but in Reg's own admission it was more akin to a Woody Allen film. He turned on the gas but left the windows open! After that the engagement was terminated, just three weeks before the planned wedding day.

As the group followed Baldry into cabaret Reg became disenchanted and sought a change. He dumped the electric piano and returned to the good old acoustic version. 'I was a vamper' he later said of his days with the Bluesology. 'I played on a

vox continental — until it died. It was a bright red beast, and one day it exploded. I used to think they were great because Alan Price played on one with the Animals. And I'm terrible on Hammond organ. It's too big for me and I'm too lazy to learn about drawbars. I'm not electrically minded at all.'

It was his dissatisfaction with the band that led him to answer an advert for new artists in the New Musical Express. Liberty Music were leaving the EMI empire and needed young talent to give them fresh products.

Reg hadn't sung for years and the only songs he knew the complete lyrics of were two by Jim Reeves. Not having performed solo since the days at the Northwood public house, he failed the audition but caught the imagination of house producer Ray Williams and he stopped the departing Reg in the lobby. In his hand he held a sheaf of lyrics from another young hopeful Bernie Taupin, who had also replied to the advert. Williams offered the sheets to Reg in the hope that something might come of a partnership. Keen to write original material but without the ability to turn his hands to words, and with a stagnating career at the tender age of twenty what did he have to lose?

In that heady year of '67 seventeen-year-old Bernie Taupin was at a crossroads. He didn't relish the prospect of a regular nine-to-five job and yet his desire to be a writer appeared impractical. A short stint as a trainee reporter on a local paper failed to match his expectations when he found himself confined to the machine room. On seeing the Liberty advert he collected a few of his poems, drafted a letter but changed his mind before posting it and threw it in the wastepaper basket. His mother discovered it there and helped the fates along by mailing it on for him.

That first batch of lyrics inspired Reg to compose songs aimed at the charts. In retrospect the material was derivative but at the time it seemed to be the starting point to something. Reg and Bernie subsequently began corresponding and Bernie sent more lyrics down from his home in Lincolnshire. The first publishing deal they signed was with the Hollies company but little came of it. However Reg picked up some session work and appeared on budget labels covering current Top Forty hits.

It was during this formative period that Reg met the main catalyst in his career. Dick James, a one time singer who had made his name by publishing The Beatles' hits, had invested his income in a songwriters demo studio in the basement of his new offices. Reg met Dick when Ray Williams of Liberty took a chance with a Reg and Bernie song *Scarecrow* and brought it to DJM studios to demo.

It was at this session that Bernie and Elton finally met face to face. Elton played his postal partner the songs he had written around the lyrics and they sealed their partnership with a handshake and a cup of coffee.

Ironically Caleb Quaye was now the engineer at the basement studio and gave Reg unlimited access, which Dick James was not too happy about. An unknown, and what is more, unsigned artist monopolising his facilities had him in two minds whether to throw them out or sign them up. His business sense won and Reg and Bernie found themselves professional songwriters.

Bernie left Lincolnshire and moved in with Reg and his parents in South London. A retainer of £10 a week was enough for them to live on and with Reg also signed as a singer the partnership went into full gear. For a year and a half they wrote top forty material but the songs lacked originality. It was a very unsatisfactory situation.

Bluesology was now a very small part of Reg's career and only the promise of recording a third single with the band postponed his departure. *Since I Found You Baby* was released on Polydor in late '67. It too flopped and he gave up the ghost and left.

Caleb produced an album's worth of the somewhat pretentious material Bernie and Elton were then writing but little came of it. The actor, Edward Woodward, chose one of the 'demos' as a single while another, *I Can't Go On Living Without You* was sung by Lulu as a 'Song for Europe'. Britain's entry in the Eurovision Song Contest however was not the John/Taupin song which was placed sixth out of six. Cilla Black later covered *I Can't Go On Living Without You* but these minor successes were very unfulfilling for the aspiring writers.

Caleb persuaded Dick James to let Reg release a single of his own through their affilliated label, Phillips. Dick agreed but with a name like Reg Dwight he was on a loser from the start. So Reg took Elton from his old sax player, Elton Dean and the surname John came up after hours of searching. And so, in the early months of 1968, Reginald Dwight became Elton John.

The song chosen for the first Elton John single was *I've Been Loving You*, released in March '68. It flopped, but they weren't short for advice. Songwriters Bill Martin and Phil Coulter took on the role of mentors and encouraged Bernie and Elton to write for themselves. Dick James however had other ideas and as he was paying their wages, Elton and Bernie continued as in-house formula writers.

Reg celebrates his new name

It was left up to the new arrival at DJM, Steve Brown, to give that little extra push necessary. Caleb Quaye had already risked his job giving Elton free studio time but it was Steve who, as the new A & R manager, had the power to give the writers their heads.

Caleb left the company just before Elton and Bernie returned with the result of their first 'serious' effort *Lady Samantha* which was exactly what Steve had asked for. A song written for themselves. Steve persuaded Dick James to allow him to produce the single which they recorded in just one evening. *Lady Samantha* was released on Dick's own label, DJM Records on 17 January 1969. A turntable hit only sold about 7000 copies and failed to make the charts.

Then interviews began to appear in the press. At first it was the local papers and then the teen magazines. In one Elton appealed for recognition as an artist and songwriter and in another he recalled his initial inspiration. 'I always wanted to be famous — the old egotist' he candidly remarked. 'It takes me about twenty minutes to write the music of a song, but Bernie spends much longer on the words'.

It was around this time that Elton began a love affair with flamboyant clothes. 'I like buying clothes, although I don't very often . . . I've got some Noddy shirts. They're made out of nursery curtain material. A neighbour made them for me.' But more of that later.

In April '69 the follow up single was recorded. In the characteristic speed of the music business of those days, it was in the shops one month later. *It's Me That You Need* was a disappointing seller. Its sales did not however deter DJM from releasing the first Elton John album *Empty Sky* on 3 June 1969. 'I remember when we had finished work on the title track' he later remarked 'I thought it was the best thing I ever heard in my life . . . it's difficult to explain the amazing enthusiasm we felt as the album began to take shape'. Caleb had been tracked down and asked to play guitar and Dee Murray and Nigel Olsson were hired for bass and drums respectively.

The album has dated somewhat. The fanciful Taupin lyrics are at times trite and the production is pedestrian but Elton's melodies stand up well. Of that first LP he later said: *Empty Sky* was low budget to say the least, we recorded it in the little four track studio downstairs. The stereo was a con, anyone who bought it as a stereo album was definitely conned'.

Steve Brown saw his own limitations as a producer and returned to plugging. It was his effort that led to good national daytime play for the

On Top of the Pops 1970

album and that in turn led to a healthy sales total of 20,000. Not bad for a debut LP by a relative unknown and without a hit single.

They gathered themselves some weighty press coverage at the time and in one interview Elton explained their modus operandi. 'Bernie writes all my lyrics and I write the songs. This has worked out well and some songwriters and artists have given us a lot of support in our efforts. Cook and Greenaway have been a great help . . . when you look at Lennon, you know that he doesn't allow the pressures to get him down. Zappa is about ten years ahead of his time. I take it all with a laugh. I mean what I'm doing but you have to look at it that way.'

'Too many of the writers and bands take this whole thing too seriously. If you're in it for the money, a bad song or a failure to make any cash will leave you considering suicide or moping around in utter despair. I admire the way commercial songwriters can churn the stuff out though, even if I don't like the songs. I just can't understand why they get so hopelessly involved with doing it. Like Tony McCauley and a load of others who try to

explain how they had tears rolling down and great spasms of emotion during the writing. You have to take some stock in creating a song, but you have to keep the whole outlook in a light vein or it becomes incredibly mechanical and loses all feeling.'

As the media became aware of a new Lennon/McCartney partnership in the making so they enquired about their past. Elton gave his version of events to date. 'Three years ago I was belting round the country backing Long John Baldry in a group called Bluesology, a soul band of ill-repute. I didn't see any future in it, we are just grinding around playing *Knock On Wood* six times a night, and I decided that I wanted to do something that didn't involve travelling and with songwriting. About then Liberty broke away from EMI and a guy called Ray Williams, who used to manage the Race and who worked for them, put an ad in the papers for songwriters. So I wrote up and said that I could write music but not lyrics and it so happened that

Bernie Taupin had written that day or rather his mother had made him write in, and said that he was a lyric writer . . . we made about fifty demos in the Dick James studios, which is a tiny little room where we recorded the first album in fact, just pottering along quite happily not bothering much about anything and then there was this enormous row when Dick found out that all three demos were being made by us and lots of other people and he threw everyone out except us. Dick said "Well you're not bad" and then we had immediate pressures to write Englebert Humperdinck type songs for about a year and a half, which we didn't really want to do and none of them were ever hits for people, anyway.'

'But eventually we got together about an album of stuff that we didn't think was too bad for the time, the time being about the start of the acid-freak-out thing. Then Steve Brown, who was a plugger from EMI came along and heard it and said, "Well really its just fucking rubbish". So we exploded of course and then sulked for two weeks, after which we thought a bit about it and went back to him, cap in hand as it were, and asked for his advice. Steve told us to forget about Dick and write just what we wanted to do.'

'The results of that little chat were *Lady Samantha* and *Skyline Pigeon* and Steve thought *Lady Samantha* would make a good 'A' side so we cut it and it was released with the result that everyone from John Peel to Jimmy Young played it on their shows. I was amazed . . .'

James believed that another album should be released as soon as possible in order to capitalise on the growing interest in Elton and to establish him as an artist of note. The next step therefore was to find a suitable producer. The first choice, George Martin, was unavailable. But *Space Oddity* arranger Paul Buckmaster suggested Bowie's producer Gus Dudgeon. Elton played him a demo of *Your Song* and Gus agreed to produce the next album. His involvement in the project also persuaded Buckmaster to reconsider the offer to be the arranger. With this impressive combination of talents Dick James allowed a budget of £6,000 for recording. Quite a risk for a relative unknown.

A lot of preparation went into the making of that eponymously titled LP with Buckmaster and Dudgeon together working hard on arrangements, while Elton continued his session work for other artists. In just four weeks twelve tracks were recorded and mixed. Two were rejected and used later as B-sides. Most of the material that required strings was recorded during one hectic week with a small orchestra. Only the vocals were then overdubbed.

'We wanted to do an album with strings a long time ago' claimed Elton 'but it took us a year to find an arranger who could really understand our music. Gus Dudgeon, who we knew was a good producer with strings, suggested Paul Buckmaster and when we met him he was exactly what we wanted. The other problem with getting this album out was that I wanted to use the band who were on the first album — can't mention any names because they're on an American label now, but they couldn't read music so Paul had to write out all the bass notes for them which took ages'.

The album was released on 10 April 1970 and immediately met with critical acclaim. Some likened it to American singer/songwriter Randy Newman and compared Elton's vocal sound with that of Stevie Wonder and Jose Feliciano. As well as the classic *Your Song* the album featured Elton's next single *Border Song*. A mixture of gospel and soul music, it builds from just piano and voice to an emotive climax courtesy of a sympathetic string arrangement and gospel choir. Critics were hard put to categorise him, preferring somewhere between the 'progressive' bands and the ligh-weight popsters. One reviewer pointed to Elton's ability to emulate the modern classical composers such as Bartok, Sibelius and Neilson.

On that second LP Elton struck a fine balance between soulful ballads and hard edged rockers. On the one hand you had the gentle but disturbing *Sixty Years On* and on the other Stones influenced *No Shoe Strings on Louise*. He dedicated one track on each of these early albums to the Stones because 'I really dig them and I suppose because I do quite a good Jagger voice.'

In the stale atmosphere of that Spring a talent as refreshingly original as Elton's was given much attention in the press but he wasn't without his critics. Some found the *Elton John* album over-produced. 'Actually I thought there'd be more criticism than there was. I was quite expecting it. I was expecting to be launched into a tirade of criticism against Buckmaster. But I really don't think that you can launch into that much of a tirade because I think that the arrangements for that album are classic.'

'So many people, and so many arrangers are going to listen to that album, and they have been. The new Bread album, for example is unlike any of the other Bread albums, although they're very heavily orchestrated. It's influencing a lot of people and they're saying "I wish I could write arrangements like Buckmaster", and nobody can, and that's the great thing about it.' The criticism was mostly that the tracks should have been allowed to stand up without all the arrangements.

Did he agree with that aspect? 'I think that's a valid criticism but I disagree, because I'm into heavy orchestration on some things. A lot of people are more into sort of basics, so am I. I mean *Empty Sky* couldn't be more basic, and I love it . . . I quite enjoy hearing *Empty Sky* on the radio.'

The album established John and Taupin as a respected songwriting team and their songs began to be covered by such diverse artists as Dusty Springfield and Toe Fat! 'It's been a knockout' Elton enthused, 'to know that people like Dusty Springfield like what we are doing. I was singing *Border Song*, the single, on *Top Of The Pops* the other day and Dusty was in the studio. She heard what we did and asked if she could so some backing singing for our future recordings. I mean, Dusty doing backing for ME! She's always been a favourite of mine anyway, and a few days later came to a Saturday session.'

And in another interview he commented on the way he and Bernie worked, before continuing with a list of their credits! 'Bernie doesn't write the lyrics as if they are coming from me. He writes for himself, but I am so much in tune with the way he thinks and feels, I know exactly how his words should be treated. Together we wrote *Lady Samantha* which, besides being my first single, was recorded by Three Dog Night on their last album which sold a million. And they are putting *Your Song*, another of our compositions, on their next album which already has a million advance orders. That makes me and my bank manager very happy indeed. Cilla Black is doing the same song as Edward Woodward, Callan on television, and the Virgil Brothers are recording other songs of ours.'

After a brief appearance at the bottom end of the Top Fifty *Border Song* sank dissapointingly out of sight. The absence of live performances may have been partly to blame; a short spot at the Round-house Pop Proms, was an abortive attempt to make some kind of showing but the glam rock onslaught was only six months away and the days of the singer/songwriter were numbered. Elton needed a band. 'There just hasn't seen the right setting or opportunity to present myself as a live act' he complained. 'Getting a band together has always been to much of a problem, although now I am seriously getting around to doing it. I remember I did a gig for some college and there was just me and the piano and all these people sitting listening. It was very nice and made me feel as though I ought to do more things like that. But when it comes to doing concert appearances and things you can forget it. At the moment it would be the height of pretentiousness. I mean, anyone can put

on a concert for themselves at the Albert Hall but there is no guarantee they would fill it unless they are an established name. I'm not.'

In the meantime work was already beginning on a new album. 'Already we're working on a double album to be released in the autumn. Most of the stuff on it will be rocking, funking materials like *Sun Of Your Father* which Spooky Tooth recorded just after he wrote it. Actually, I swear I'm a rocker at heart. Our one misgiving about *Elton John* was that when people heard it was done with vast orchestras they would think we had sold out or something. But perhaps what hasn't been realised until lately is that orchestrated music can have loads of guts and fire. We are proud of this one and the arrangement on *Sixty Years On* by Paul is really quite something else. A lot of the way it's been done is classical or quite near it!'

Not all of the cover versions pleased them however. In an interview at the time Bernie Taupin listed the bands who couldn't be bothered to make sure they had the correct lyrics before recording the song!

'The trouble is' said Bernie, 'that they never believe the words I write anyway, so they change them to suit themselves! Unfortunately there are so very few British groups that I can have any respect for. Everyone's still playing variations of The Cream's riffs and there's no new groups coming along with anything like the originality or the presence of the American groups such as Spirit and The Band.'

It was an aggravating situation that Elton later expanded upon.

'We never write for anyone else in fact, although some other people, like Three Dog Night and Toe Fat have used some of our songs. In fact Three Dog Night used three on their last album, which is keeping us eating at the moment! But no-one really does the songs as we'd like them, tho' Toe Fat did quite a nice job with *Bad Side Of The Moon*. The main trouble is that they keep getting things wrong. Three Dog Night made one of the chords in the chorus of *Lady Samantha* a D-minor instead of a major. The worst thing is the new Silver Metre album, on which there are three of our numbers and one of them, *Ballad of a Well Known Gun* we just didn't recognise as being one of ours! They've called it "Now they've found me", or something, and they've altered one line from "Now I know how Reno felt when he ran from the Law" to "Now I know how Enoch felt when he ran from the Law"!'

Despite having their songs recorded (accurately or not!) the album was an anti-climax, as far as sales went. 'It was a flop' Elton admitted. 'We were expecting great things but all that happened was

that a lot of the songs got recorded by other people.' The pressure to form a band and take to the road was not too great to be put off any longer. Steve Brown approached bass player Dee Murray and drummer Nigel Olsson who had just left the Spencer Davis group. Both left their current

As Elton's hair recedes, he starts his long love affair with hats

subordinate positions in lightweight MOR groups and began rehearsals with Elton. From now on things would be different.

2 MADMAN WATER

The Elton John band, Elton, Nigel and Dee, went into rehearsals in the spring of 1970 and from day one Elton knew that this was it. 'I couldn't have wished for a better band . . . I can't say I did expect to find such good sidemen as Nigel and Dee. There was all this pressure on me to get a group together and I had to do it.

'I had a pretty clear idea of the kind of group it should be, you know the basic, raw thing . . . lots of power. But knowing that, I also thought it would very nearly impossible to get just the right people for the job. When Dee came along I knew he was it, it had to be. I knew what he could do, how he would contribute and I had to have him. But Nigel was a different case.

'I was a little bit unsure about him at the start, but I didn't say anything because I wanted to give him a chance to prove himself. I thought I saw something there. Other people said to get rid of him because they thought he wasn't good enough, but I said "Hold on, wait", and it's worked because he's improved so much it's just not true. I don't think he knows to this day that he might have been out if I had listened to the others, but it's nice to think they've had to chew all those opinions.

'Nigel had just been a pop drummer, he's much more now . . . oh, another point about keeping Nigel was that he could sing, that was very important. Both Nigel and Dee sing very well, it's one of our strengths.'

The first engagement offered to the band was the support slot on a Sergio Mendes European tour. 'They aren't exactly my scene' Elton admitted 'so I just hope the audiences will accept us both. On the continent, though, they are inclined to mix up the bills. It's quite a good experience, I suppose. I hope to be going to the States in June. I'd really love to go there.'

But the Mendes tour was a no-hoper from the start. Mendes hated the band from the first night and paid them off not to complete the tour! However, the clouds of gloom were soon dispelled by the offer of an appearance on *Top Of The Pops* together with an itinerary for a showing of

18

ACROSS THE

dates in the U.K. 'I'd really like to do a couple of gigs a week, because that's how you sell yourself to people. *Top Of The Pops* doesn't really give anybody an idea of what you can do . . . in fact it gives them a totally wrong impression.'

'It's nice to be getting into the live thing again. It's strange, after all these years of being a backing musician it's really odd to be the leader of a band. I've got to start thinking of the visual side of the act again. We're not entirely a visual act, you're very limited on piano, still we've got a very visual drummer. In fact I'm very pleased with the band.'

The college circuit was still the haven of the rising singer/songwriters and Elton found the students more responsive. 'We really started last month, which is a bit unfortunate really as the colleges where we do most of our gigs have broken up. The band is really nice — I play piano and there's Dee Murray on bass and Nigel Olsson on drums. We're trying to get away from the guitar thing as much as we can. Caleb Quayle, who plays guitar on the album has got his own band together. There's such a lot to do — songwriting, gigging and recording — it's quite a strain.

'So far we've had a great reception, we've played two bummers but even then the audience reaction was good. We prefer the North to London. London audiences are very blasé, they have so much music to choose from that they tend to forget they're there to enjoy themselves. In the North people go out with enjoyment in their minds, being cool is of less importance to them.

'I hope I will appeal to all audiences. I don't want to be tied down to a certain type of music because it just becomes a drag after a while. And if you do something different then people will start saying that you've changed, when all the time you haven't really!

'At the moment, I probably appeal more to the underground type rather than the young ones because they can't really dance or rave to my songs — they have to listen to them. We don't sit down and compose for any particular type of people. You could call us unpretentious. We just do what we want to do and hope that everyone will listen.'

Drummer Nigel Olsson was somewhat frustrated and remarked 'Not many people seem to realise that Elton John has these other guys with him.' But Elton and Bernie were keen for the band to work and create as a unit and not for it to be just a singer/songwriter with a piano and a backing band mechanically following the songs dot for dot. 'Once the song's done we all get together on the arrangements'. Nigel continued 'the lyrics and melodies are never changed, but we all throw

ideas on how to do the songs — there's no big argument scene. Elton has the most say, of course, but it never comes to that, there's no "I'm the boss" thing.'

The second album had sold well in the States and Uni Records were anxious to have the band undertake a short promotional tour. A schedule was drawn up and September 1970 was pencilled in for the visit. '. . . in September we've got a tour of the States coming off. Already most of our money comes from the States, they're much more aware of us over there than they are here. We're going to be playing at the Troubadour in Los Angeles.'

'I'm looking forward to it because I'm much more into American bands than British bands. Most of the British bands are hung up on loud guitars and tight trousers, they're just a flash. All the American bands stay together for such a long time and really get into each other. Bands like Spirit, Airplane, Steve Miller, The Band and the old Buffalo Springfield create so much atmosphere, they concentrate on communication rather than being pop stars.

'Britain also seems to be devoid of songwriters at the moment. America's got Nilsson, Joni Mitchell, Steve Stills, Neil Young — I'm sure it's going to be a much more creative environment over there.'

Just before embarking on the American tour Elton was filmed for a BBC television series on the new breed of British singer/songwriters. It would be shown after his return from the States and add to the cult status of the new phenomonen who was still to have a hit.

'Television gives you massive exposure for records, but I'm convinced that working to live audiences is the best way to build up a reputation. Any sort of fame I might have had has been built up by word of mouth . . . people saying to their friends, "you must go and see Elton John, he's not at all bad", or "have you heard Elton John's new album? I'll lend it to you for a couple of days". That's how it seems to have happened, and as far as I'm concerned, that's the best way.

'We've done quite a bit of television lately. We've done a whole show for Belgian Television, and in September we've got a BBC 2 show going on. It's a series called *In Concert*, it's being produced by Stanley Dorfmann, there's thirteen in the series and each one features a performer/ composer. They've got such people as Leonard Cohen and Joni Mitchell, so I was really knocked out when I was asked to do one as well.

At Shepperton Studios rehearsing with the band, 'China' 1977

'Actually the BBC has been quite nice to me. It's on Radio One almost every day, and the fact that John Peel and Jimmy Young play my stuff is very pleasing. I want to get through to as wide an audience as possible.'

It is not generally known that Elton was on the verge of giving up just before that first American tour. Jeff Beck had invited Elton to join his band as piano player and Elton was sorely tempted. 'Before we got the offer to go, I was on the point of packing it all in and joining Jeff Beck, believe it or not. But that fell through, and we went to the States expecting nothing at all.'

Elton later amended the facts to suit his superstar status and assured the press that it was Beck who wanted to join his band and not the other way around. '. . . and by quirk of fate, I got a band together and we were beginning to do okay . . . we were beginning to build the name Elton John gradually in England, and then we could either have gone over to Los Angeles to do the Troubadour club or . . . I got approached at the last minute by Jeff Beck, who saw us one night at the Speakeasy in London and said "Listen I want to join your band". So I said "Alright". I was a bit wary at first, I said "A thousand watts of guitar, I can't stand it".

'I really wanted the group to be just piano, bass and drums. Anyway, I said '"Well, come and do an audition"', so he came down and he was fine. He played very quietly and very tastefully, and then he said, '"well, I'm sorry, but I want to throw out your drummer,"' and I made it plain that he was going to meet with violent opposition from me.'

And then he wanted to employ me, he wanted me to come and do a tour of the States and pay me money to be in his band, 10 per cent of what he was going to earn, and the original idea was for him to join our band. So it was either going to be join him; or come to L.A., so we thought '"Sod Jeff Beck, we'll go to L.A."' and we did, and we were really glad that we stuck on that because that's where we got lucky . . .'

Whether luck played any part in that make-or-break tour no one knows but they were certainly in the right place at the right time. DJM had hired a doubledecker London bus to meet the band at the airport and drive them through to Los Angeles to the amusement of the residents. For all the showbiz razzamatazz that was used to hype Elton in the States the imported copies of *Empty Sky* and the American pressings of the *Elton John* had been generating a genuine buzz on the West Coast.

Elton John played a showcase gig at the prestigious Troubadour club in California on 25 August 1970. The audience was in the main made up of industry people; agents, promoters, disc jockeys and all had been cleverly wound up by the promotion team at Uni Records. From the moment he strode on stage to begin *Your Song* he had it made. In the most famous tradition of the theatre he had walked on an unknown and come back a star!

The diverseness of the set, from whispering ballads to screaming rockers, were delivered with the conviction of an established performer. Despite his relative inexperience he was compelling to watch, a natural performer. Elton himself described the tour and that night in particular, as 'phenomenal'. And he added 'I never imagined anything like it. Uni — our record company in the States arranged for us to go over because they felt that it was the right time. They really did a great job, they looked after us and promoted us as good business people should.

'Every place we played we received a standing ovation and the newspaper critics never ceased showering us with praise. As far as I was concerned the gig we did in Philadelphia was the best because it was playing to kids instead of a sophisticated audience, and they really dug us.

'The Americans were outrageous; they gave me this big 'superstar' build up and by the end of three weeks I felt very depressed and shattered. They tended to ignore Bernie, who usually travels with me, which annoyed me but he didn't mind much — he fell in love while he was over there, and that compensates for everything, doesn't it?'

'What pleased me most was the crowd that came to see me at the Troubadour in Los Angeles; lots of press people and dee-jays. Graham Nash, Quincey Jones, and Leon Russell stayed for both sets which knocked me out and the next day we all went down to his house and jammed and listened to tapes.'

In three weeks they cracked the hardest market first, and all without a U.K. hit! But he hadn't given up hope on that one yet. 'It's just a case of waiting until Bernie Taupin, who writes the lyrics to my tunes, and I come up with the right song.' He was now determined to return to England and break down the walls of indifference.

'I've only had my band together for a few months — Dee Murray on bass, Nigel Olssen on drums and me on piano — we did a few gigs, mostly colleges and clubs, before we went to America. We're really going to get out and play to the public in the future.

'It's a real band now, and the boys have helped me a lot. It's so tight now but in a year's time it'll be unbelievable. America did our confidence a lot of good, and I don't ever have to tell them what to do, because we all know what we're doing. There are some songs with very broken rhythms, but they just play them without having it explained to them.'

On his return a planned tour of Scotland was cancelled to make way for a second assault on the States, only a one-nighter at the Royal Albert Hall in London remained on the schedule. He threatened to wear a gold lamé tail-suit. 'It's from a Thirties Busby Berkeley musical . . . I might sew some sausages on it for the occasion.' After the gig he admitted 'The Albert Hall the other night was much too big and the sound was terrible. I don't think anyway that I've heard anyone but Crosby, Stills, Nash and Young sound good there. But then you learn by your mistakes, we'd never play it again.'

'I'd like to work here a lot more but at the moment things are very slow here and I might as well go to America where the grass is greener. There were some incredible scenes last time and I can't wait to get back.' He expressed doubts about 'deserting England', but the state of the media was now beginning to get antagonistic towards him which was further cause for concern.

'Over here the scene is all these people slaggin' Ten Years After week after week for makin' so much money and being no good. I don't like them myself but they must get pretty pissed off after a while. The States is a whole other feeling. Leon Russell is my idol — ever since the Delaney and Bonnie albums. He came to see us and I went to his house in L.A. He's got a whole recording studio there, and he told me he wanted to record *Burn Down The Mission*. His house is called the mission and his record company won't grant him insurance on it because it's in a fire area. So I don't think he'll be recording it soon.'

And in another interview he admitted he was still 'star struck' especially by Leon Russell. 'He's my idol as far as piano playing, and there he was sitting in the front row. My legs turned to jelly . . . I mean, to compare my playing with his is sacrilege. He'd eat me for breakfast. But he said that he wants to record with us, and he told me that he'd written *Delta Lady* after hearing one of our songs, which was a gas. Really, it's worth five million good reviews if someone you respect as a musician comes up and tells you they like what you're doing.'

There was no way he would lose the enthusiasm of that first tour. Even weeks later he was still on an unbelievable high. 'From the moment we arrived

Elton's first visit to Watford Football Club in November 1973

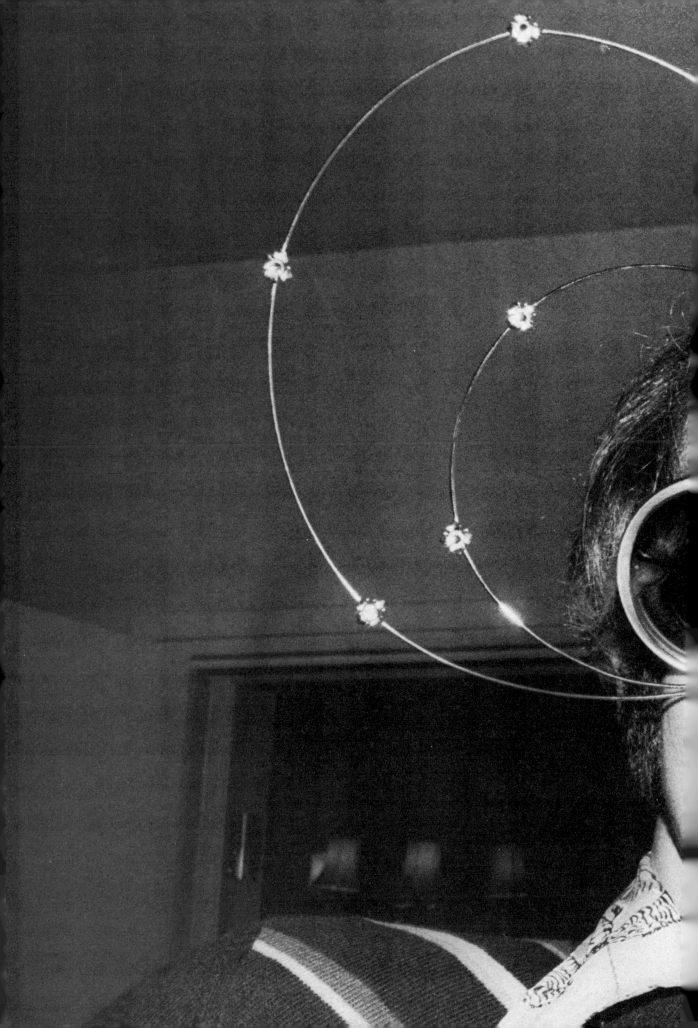

it was just pandemonium all the way. The first night at the Troubadour was hype night, with all the record company people and the press, and the first set was incredible and it stayed that way. We got unbelievable reviews — I didn't see one bad one.'

Only one month was allowed to pass between that first historic trip and a second more audacious tour. In the interim Elton and Bernie were putting the finishing touches to their third album; the very American *Tumbleweed Connection*, and adding their contribution to the soundtrack of the film *Friend*.

And so it was that Elton, Bernie and the band returned to the States in late October. They began by playing the West Coast but as they moved East the audiences grew colder. Word hadn't spread as quickly and new names were always greeted with reservation anyway. An industry showcase at the Playboy Club in New York was the first real damp squib of his American career and it took him some time to recover.

It was mainly due to bad billing; he had simply been booked to appear too late in the proceedings when most of the invited audience of journalists and record executives had filtered home or had other commitments elsewhere. Ignoring the incident in subsequent interviews Elton merely played down the disappointment.

'San Francisco audiences are a little cool at first, like those in London, because they've seen everything, and one night it was like pushing over a brick wall very slowly, but they went in the end. Los Angeles is like home for us, and Philly and Boston are great too. Every audience is good if you get at them the right way.

'There's one thing though — I'm a bit homesick. We don't seem to have seen England at all this year, and I'm looking forward to getting home on 12 December. A performance in Santa Monica was recorded for a thirty minute TV special and some of the numbers were included in a *Henry Mancini Spectacular*.

'We played for nearly two hours there,' recalled Elton 'we seem to go on longer in America than in Britain, because the audiences are so incredible. They don't vary at all, and since we played Troubadour in L.A. on the first trip we've had a standing ovation at every gig, including the ones in England in between.'

A Studio bound show for New York radio was performed for live transmission and also recorded for a possible future live LP. 'We recorded it in 8-track stereo, and we should get a good live album out of it. Mind you, it went over the air in good two-track, so there were probably millions of people sitting at home taping it for bootlegs. But it's a fantastic tape, the best playing we've ever done.'

The thrill of meeting Leon Russell on the first tour and then being given equal billing with him on the second was bettered by a meeting with The Band. Robbie Robertson had been a hero of Bernie's for a long time. 'Bernie was shaking with fear,' Elton remembered 'but they were really sweet and we talked together for about three hours. Then came the most incredible thing, because the day after we said goodbye to them and set off for Philadephia, while they went in the opposite direction, north to upstate New York. Anyway, we played a fantastic gig in Philly and when we got into our dressing room afterwards, the whole Band was there. They'd put their show forward a couple of hours, and flew down in their private plane to see our act.'

'We played *Tumbleweed Connection* to them, and they went berserk. It was such a compliment that I couldn't believe it. They asked us to go up to Woodstock to record at their place, and when Robbie Robertson asked us to write a song for them . . . well, I think Bernie was a bit embarrassed, because Robbie's his current idol.

'I've never written anything specifically for another singer before,' he said 'and we're playing the Fillmore East tonight with Leon. He's hurt his ribs so he's a bit immobile, but he's got a good band with a couple of chick singers. We're planning to do a thing in which we do our respective acts and then I go on stage and we play the piano together.'

New York, however, was a far less attractive proposition and if it were not for the prestigious venues it is unlikely he would even have passed through. 'It stinks. It really smells, the whole city seemed to have gone off. It was really terrible. Everybody who lives there keeps apologising for it. New Yorkers get really upset about what's happening to the city but they say it just gets worse and worse.' And the people? 'They were mostly very nice and pretty intelligent. But I can see that I obviously found them interesting because they were interested in my music.'

He didn't warm to the American people in general though. 'They seem to have some sort of mental block as a nation. They look for a deep motive in a shallow pool.' So, for all the success he was not planning to stay in the U.S. 'I don't think I could stand the pace or the violence. That's the worst thing about the country. The first night we were there we were woken up by a gun battle going on in the street outside our hotel. There was some guy and a policeman shooting at each other.'

With members of Watford Football Club

On his return he completed the *Friend* soundtrack. The Lewis Gilbert film, about two young children discovering first love, was to make little impact on release but while engaged on the project Elton was still enthusiastic. 'Films frighten me and when they approached us about doing this one I had to think hard. Mostly they're just a case of the writer finishing the thing and getting his money and the producers, not interested in the slightest about the music, marketing the thing to get *theirs*, but it was different with this case, because we liked what they showed us.

'It'll come out a soundtrack album, and I think there'll be a single from it, either the title song, or *Michelle's Song*. I don't want them to pull a single off my next proper album — there are no singles on it anyway.' The next 'proper' album was in fact *Tumbleweed Connection*. It had been culled from many hours of tape recorded at short bursts over a long period. It stood as a stronger collection because of this.

Just before its release in October 1970 he commented 'The next album is going to be much more like we are live. We have been accused of overproducing the last album. Some say there's too much strings on it. The next one features only four tracks with strings, the rest of the album is very funky.

'Whereas the last album was completed in the space of about a week, the new one has being recorded over a long time. All the numbers have been written by myself and Bernie Taupin, apart from one which was written by Lesley Duncan — she's a session singer who writes some very nice songs.'

Tumbleweed with its heavy Americana influence was a more determined and satisfying release. The solid mesh of piano and rhythm section was topped by the controlled but emotive vocal style that had become sharpened by the recent tour experience.

Elton described the album as 'a lot more gospelly than we've done before.' And he and Bernie were brimming with ideas fueled by pressures bearing down on them at an even greater rate, but they didn't have time to write. 'Bernie came back from America with a whole lot of ideas for an album; you can't help but being influenced by the country and what's going on there. And Bernie plans to make a spoken album of his own. He's thought about it for some time but we just haven't had time to get down to it.'

'We don't really have an awful lot of time to write and record; not since America.' Bernie was always obsessed with the Wild West, collecting books on the subject and also guns.

He described *Tumbleweed* as their 'Americana album'. 'It dealt very heavily with the Civil War and a lot of my interests in Americana came out in that album. When we did that album it wasn't really meant to have a theme, it was just that all the songs we did for that album ended up having that feel to them so it ended up being a slight concept. So I think that if I do an album myself later in the year, if it does have a theme it'll have a western theme.'

'It's something I've always wanted to get off my chest, to write a script for a western, and have something to do with the filming of it. That's why I'd probably do the theme around Sam Bass who's my own particular interest as far as outlaws are concerned and he's one of the more obscure ones and I'd like to do something around him.'

'I collect anything I can find. Obviously I find everything in America and books on the West are very hard to find here because there's no market for it. Even in America you have to go to very select places like old American bookshops — like last time I was in America I drove from L.A. to Mississippi so I went through places like Tombstone and San Antonio, and although it's a tourist's trap, it's the only place you find good books so obviously I just bought cart-loads of books and now I've gathered together a really good library.

'I love my western books and I'm just going to keep on building up a library, and as far as replicas guns and so on goes I just collect them when I see them, anything that bears any relevance and I can hang up.' As far as films go does Bernie have a favourite? 'Yeah, well there's various; Sergio Leone's *Once Upon A Time In The West* is probably one of the best westerns ever made, a lot of the old stuff like *High Noon* ... actually my favourite western is one that nothing ever happened with, it's a film called *The Great Northfield Minnesota Raid* which deals with Jesse James' collaboration with the Younger brothers. It was an amazing film which ended up being a 'B' film in the States.'

Elton's influences were somewhat different. 'Our influences change all the time, obviously, but right now I'd say I listen to a lot of James Taylor and Randy Newman, and Bernie is flashed on Robbie Robertson of The Band. You can easily hear that by listening to his lyrics. He used to be heavily into Dylan.

'I'm very happy with the new album, much more the way I want to come over, the last album was a little too soft and too orchestrated for me. Paul Buckmaster is arranging for us again and he is just totalling amazing. He's doing the most incredible things with straight session musicians. Half the time I just don't believe it. He has them all hitting their violins for three bars *and* they all love it. He is really freaky and very good. I'm so pleased that he's doing our album.

'I'm just happy producing songs as we are, even with all the influences, 'cos I don't give a shit for anybody. We have a completely free hand with all our stuff and I couldn't work any other way now. I don't have to do anything that I don't like. You just have to refuse things and be firm. At the moment I'm still struggling to get rid of this image that media like Radio One has built up for me, you know, people think that I'm all cuddly and lovely and beautifully pop-starrish. I'm not, really I'm not.'

Side one of *Tumbleweed* begins with the up-tempo stomper of *Ballad Of A Well Known Gun*. Caleb Quayle's guitar licks flit in and out of the gutsy Stones influenced riff. The track is typical of the overall positive mood of the album, in stark contrast to the brooding pessimism of its predecessor, *Elton John*. It was a timely release for it captured the essence of American tradition just as he and Bernie were being taken to U.S. hearts as the new Lennon and McCartney.

Come Down in Time is one of the few quiet tracks. A sensitive lilting ballad, it features some fine acoustic guitar playing and understated orchestration. It insinuates itself into your soul in a clever way but never cloys.

Country Comfort is similar in arrangement to Rod Stewart's cover version but Elton opted for the more authentic American feel. Rod's approach was fundamentally English and opinion is still divided as to which is the better. Despite developing a good friendship with Rod later on, Elton's reaction to Rod's version was initially hostile.

'... we're really pissed off about it. He sounds like he made it up as they played. I mean they couldn't possibly have got farther away from the original if they'd sung *Camptown Races*. It's so bloody sad because if anyone should sing that song it ought to be him, such a great voice, but now I can't even listen to the album I get so brought down. Every other word is wrong.

At Lords playing for the Vic Lewis Showbiz Eleven in a benefit match, June, 1973

'It's so frustrating man 'cos all anyone has to do is ring up the office and there are file copies of all our songs in the desk and they are welcome to have the lyrics. Silver Meter have done about four of our songs on an album that's out in the States and they are all the bloody same, so wrong so totally wrong. Dorothy Morrison has done *Border Song* as a single in the States but I still don't know of anyone that has done one of our numbers that has made me stop and say yeah, you know. You would think someone would be able to get it together and get our lyrics right. Spooky Tooth's *Son of Your Father* was an abortion, it makes me very upset when people just can't be bothered to do things right.'

The 'White-soul' of *Tumbleweed* is characterised by the track *Son Of Your Father*, again built upon a Stones feel and complete with droning harmonica. Images of the West are again in evidence on *My Father's Gun*, a splendid tale of revenge set against the background of New Orleans.

Where To Now, St. Peter is held together well by an atmospheric arrangement and sits well in the overall concept of the LP. Lesley Duncan's *Love Song* is the odd one out. Apart from being the only track not written by Elton and Bernie it is also out of step with the rest of the album.

The penultimate tracks *Amoreena* and *Talking Old Soldiers* contrast well. *Amoreena* is another funky number 'It's country rock band style' said Bernie 'as opposed to country rock Matthews Southern Comfort style.' *Old Soldiers* is just Elton and piano, reflective and intense. Possibly one of the most under-rated of the Taupin/John compositions.

The album closes with what was Elton's big number *Burn Down The Mission*. It held the rest of the LP together and closed it in much the same way as *A Day In The Life* closed *Sgt. Pepper*. A stroke of genius. Pure and simple. The coda about 'loving your brother' was added by Elton, one of the few times he added to Taupin's lyrics. He claimed it was necessary to add meaning to the rest of the verses which were rather cryptic, though in retrospect it is Elton's lines that are trite and clichéd.

Both men were very pleased with the LP and felt it had been necessary to release a funky album after the serious and deep thinking *Elton John* because there was a danger of Elton being labelled with James Taylor, Randy Newman and the like.

'It may surprise quite a lot of people but if I'd done another orchestral album I reckon I'd have been labelled for the rest of my life.' The previous two albums were also deceptive when shown against the live E.J. 'People think I'm going to be this little fellow on stage with a huge orchestra. They still don't really know what I look like or what to expect. I suppose it's a mystique in a way. People say "Oh yes, Elton John — but what does he look like?"'

'There's two distinct sides to me, that why I like doing 'Honky Tonk Woman' on stage. I look forward to that bit of rave up all evening.' 1971 was the year Elton finally broke through in England. *Your Song* was the single that made the breakthrough possible. Originally recorded a year earlier and released on the *Elton John* album in April 1970, it had been put forward as a single many times but DJs felt that at four minutes it was just too long. However, after nine months of DJs featuring it as an album cut, became a massive hit.

It's surprising then in February of '71 to hear him talking of retirement! 'My career is gonna be very short. One and a half years, that's all. I want to quit while I'm at the top and then I'll fade into obscurity. I've got lots of obligations for this year and next and when they're all done the group will split. Does it sound bad saying I want to quit while I'm at the top? I don't mean it arrogantly, it's just that so many artists never see the end, they never know when they've got that long slide ahead of them.

'We've got two more American tours this year, one early in '72 and that'll be it. There won't be anything after that, because I know, I just know, that I'll be tired of being on the road by then.

'At the moment all I'm interested in is playing because I'm enjoying myself so much. There's been all this talk about films and things, but that will come later. When the group breaks up — it must sound horrible talking about it like this, but it's so inevitable, we all accept it and that's the best way — then Nigel will go into production almost full time, I think. He prefers it to playing, it's more interesting for him. He's having great fun making his solo album at the moment, and I'm sure it's good though I haven't heard anything yet.

'Dee will always play. I can't ever see a time be, and he'll always be successful. He'd be working on his own album, too, if he could get some studio time but there's none available at the moment. He has to use Dick's studio, you see, because Dick likes everyone there. He's funny about things like that. There are just so many people in there at the moment there's no time. It's different for superstars like me of course (sniggers). I've got so used to Trident and IBC that I couldn't use anywhere else.'

An early publicity picture

It's strange to read that statement now. So many of his plans were changed as he was caught up in the rat race that passes as the music business. His career was extended to six years before he officially announced retirement and even now he is still releasing products and doing selected dates. The group continued, albeit in amended form for another seven years and Elton recorded in many studios over his long and distinguished career.

IBC was the studio he used to produce an album by his old mate Long John Baldry. The blues singer had met with financial problems and both Elton and Rod Stewart agreed to help out, each producing one side of his new LP.

Their approaches differed greatly. '. . . I'm very impatient. When I record I like to have things done straight away. Rod's probably different to me. I did all mine in twenty hours. I recorded the back tracks, the voice, the overdubs, the choir, the mixing . . . it was all done in twenty hours, and I had enough for one side of an album and more.

'Rod took ages, one night a number, if I can't do anything in ten minutes or twenty minutes . . . that's why I can never play another instrument, because if I can't master something I just forget it. I'm really into touring and playing to live people . . .

'You can probably tell it's me who produced it. It's the first thing I'd produced. I didn't think I could produce a record and I'm very pleased at the way it's come out. I'm very pleased with it because I thought that I would be a disastrous producer, because I am so impatient.

'Rod's side turned out raucous, with drums sounding like kettles . . . Rod's side sounds very much like *Gasoline Alley* and my side sounds like Mantovani. I'm on that sort of thing. I'm more into choirs and things like that, and Rod's into . . . it's good because both sides of the album are different. My side is very polished and Rod's side is very raucous and probably how John should sound. I'll probably get attacked for it.

'He's a great blues singer. He hasn't got that good technically a voice but he's got a great, deep blues voice. And he started the whole scene up in England anyway. He just got to the point where he was going to the cabaret clubs singing things like *Malagania*. I mean, there was no need, and I was getting brassed off, and all of a sudden I got this phone call from his manager saying "Will you do an album?" Well I said "anything as long as it's not *Let the Heartaches Begin* or something with a ninety-piece orchestra."

'I can't get a tune out of this!'

'John's very sort of headstrong and gets mad ideas, and he wanted to do things like Peggy Lee's *Is That All There Is* and Rod and I kind of said "now listen here young man." It's been very strange to do an album for him when I used to be his organ player.

'It really did very weird things to me. But I'm very glad of the way it's turned out, because he deserved more than he got. Look at the musicians that have been associated with him. It reads à la John Mayall. He was going before John Mayall wore napkins.'

April saw the release of two LP's *Friends* and the 'live' LP *17-11-70*. An audience of 100 invited guests had been witness to that historic Elton John session at the studios of WABC in New York City. Elton had been so pleased with the spirited performance and the intimate atmosphere that Steve Brown had captured on tape that he immediately sanctioned an official release of the concert.

WABC-FM was a leading influence on what was later to be termed the AOR audience (adult or album orientated rock) and New Yorkers in the know were tuned in to catch the name WABC was giving its stamp of approval to. Ironically they were also armed with tape recorders and Elton later blamed subsequent bootlegs for depriving him of 100,000 sales on the official release.

The three-piece breathed fire into the inherent power of *Burn Down The Mission*, *Take Me To The Pilot* and rock standards *My Baby Left Me*, *Get Back* and *Honky Tonk Woman*. It was simply a performance without the frills associated with Paul Buckmaster's string arrangement or Gus Dudgeon's studio trickery. *17-11-70* was Elton at his raunchy, raw best.

Friends, the soundtrack that Elton and Bernie had initially entered with enthusiasm had turned sour mid-way through recording. Film makers and rock artists apparently did not make good working partners. In the end two tracks left over from the *Tumbleweed Connection* sessions were included. *Honey Roll* and *Can I Put You On?* The former was a solid little funky number and the latter a quickly assembled filler typifying a very scrappy and overblown album.

Despite the quality of *Friends* and the growing proliferation of John product the albums sold exceptionally well in the States. The Americans had a vociferous appetite for E.J. material and all four LPs had, by the spring of '71, gone gold. At one point he had all four albums in the Top Forty, a feat unequalled since the heyday of The Beatles. Elton John was now an established artist. And his new album was awaited with bated breath.

3 AT THE H CHATEAU

In the interim period between the release of *17-11-70* and the much maligned *Madman Across The Water* (the sixth album in just two and a half years!) came Bernie Taupin's pet project. An eponymous album of original poetry spoken over mundane mood music provided by Caleb, Davey and Shawn Phillips, it was not a good seller.

Bernie had written most of the poems during the recording of the *Elton John* album and decided to release them on record in order to establish himself as a poet as against an easily pigeon-holed rock lyricist. Bernie was also a very good short story writer and over the following years often spoke of his intentions to publish collections of stories and poems for children. In 1972 he was still working on a epic fantasy poem called *Warlords of the Marshlands* together with a fairy story. 'I've spent more time on that than anything for a long time' he confessed. 'I spend hours and hours rewriting a verse. Its the best stuff I've ever written so far.'

Elton however was growing restless with the singer/songwriter tag and saw the imminent decline of that particular breed. His stage shows were becoming brash rock and roll circus, almost vaudeville on occasion, with energetic assaults upon the keyboard in true Little Richard style and a growing wardrobe of outrageous clothes. It's a quirk he attributes to 'a bad childhood . . . I was fat, about two hundred pounds, and I had a terrible inferiority complex . . . I'm catching up for all the games that I missed as a child.'

It was obvious to everyone that the orchestrated albums were sounding dated on release and that the rock and roll revival was under way. It's hard to imagine the state of the music industry back in 1971 in the current climate of techno-rock and colourful electronic dance music. But when Elton John was recording his last fully orchestrated album *Madman*, his nearest 'rivals' were the manufactured cabaret pop bands like Middle of the Road, Lieutenant Pigeon and The New Seekers.

The Beatles had split, and rock had become

ONKY

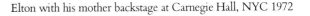

stale. The potential singles buying market was ignored altogether and heavy rock seemed the only alternative. Then along came Marc Bolan. Bolan claimed to have lifted his taste in clothes from Mae West, with a bias in favour of gold suits as worn by Elvis Presley on the cover of one of his records. He was reported to be spending several hundred pounds a time on clothes and he took to wearing make-up with a touch of glitter under his eyes. Bolan irreverently kicked away the old values and brought fun back into pop. For Elton it came not a moment too soon.

'T. Rex and Rod Stewart's albums are the best rock albums I've heard all year — just raw, raucous rock'n'roll. I think one becomes too polished and the awful thing is that there are no bloody young musicians bringing that energy back into music. Free were about the only new band that were doing it and they went and split up.'

As Bolan struggled on his own to resurrect the art of the three minute pop single so the pretentious neo-classical rock bands and over serious singer/songwriters buried their heads in the sand. Elton complained 'The rock scene is stagnating in Britain. Since I've been back the only three new albums I've liked have been from America, Lindisfarne, and Yes. There's so much rubbish around. Music has become too technical and precise — I think I've been to blame too as far as records are concerned. It's lost all that lovely rawness.'

'Now it's just a job and everyone's saying "Oh how much advance are we getting on the album". There's no magic left. I mean James Taylor's the biggest name in the world but he's not really exciting, he's a bit of a wet fish really to see live. I'm sure this is the reason festivals are dying — who do you put on to draw real crowds?'

'The last two festivals I went to were Dylan at the Isle of Wight and The Stones in Hyde Park. They hit directly they came on stage. But the big artists that have come up in the last couple of years just don't have that same identification. Fairport are very entertaining and I like watching them, so are The Faces and T. Rex. That's about it. Marc Bolan is

35

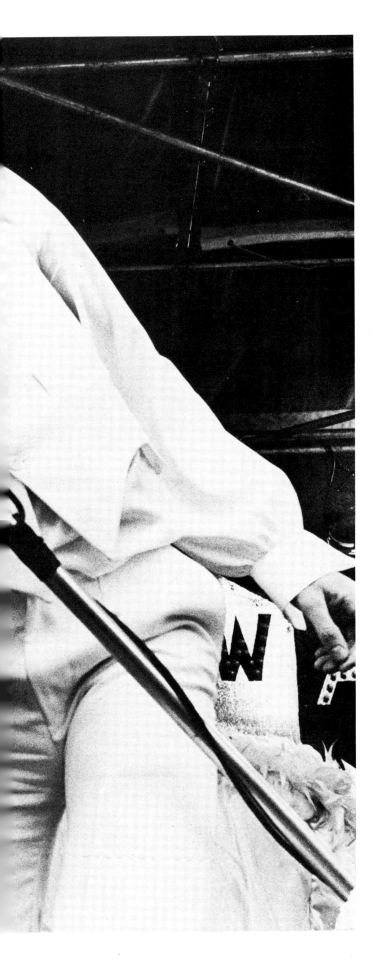

really our only hope if he can keep it up and forget about the knocks — and how long's it taken Rod Stewart for God's sake?

'These people are the new sex idols if you like, and it's just as well they're around. Well I'm not, that's for sure. I don't know where I belong.' His obvious confusion was further tested with the release of the new album on 5 November 1971. The finely orchestrated tracks were in direct opposition to the mood of the time and he suffered at the hands of the critics.

'That kind of thing does upset me. I got very upset for the first couple of weeks and then the criticism reached a very bitchy level. I don't mind album criticism which can often be helpful, but when they started saying things like Lesley Duncan's album was okay even though I was on it — well that's being bloody evil for the sake of it.

'The sad thing is that I've gone out of my way to be nice to everyone and I end up getting kicked in the teeth for it. Everything gets so out of hand in Britain. I mean all the dressing up started as a joke, something for a laugh, a spontaneous thing, and people have taken it seriously. They must be joking, mustn't they? The only thing about stopping the leaping about is that I think it stopped being spontaneous. I mean everyone knows now that at a certain point in the evening I'll kick the stool away and go into frenzied antics. It's wearing a bit thin — it is for me anyway.

'I mean I got slagged off for my sense of humour and the sense of humour I brought into stage clothes and now look what's happening everywhere in music — with eyeshadow added! The funny thing is that I think I'm out and then I play Manchester or somewhere and nearly get torn off stage — little teenybopper Reg! In the end you don't know what to think about your standing.

'The thing that bugs me most is that I don't think I've ever got credit for influencing so many things — the clothes thing, strings on albums. Even Lennon used strings on *Imagine* very akin to the way we always used them. I'm very aware of what goes on — I follow everyone like a hawk!'

Madman Across The Water was made under a great deal of pressure and with more than its fair share of problems. Paul Buckmaster couldn't work under pressure and Elton was becoming frus-

(above) Elt 'n' Rod

(Pages 36 & 37) Two faces of Elton, the snappy dresser

trated with the numerous disappointments. One day Buckmaster arrived to find sixty string players waiting to begin work and he hadn't brought a score! 'There were all sorts of these disasters' Elton later remarked, somewhat embittered by the experience.

However it did feature guitarist Davey Johnstone for the first time, an addition Elton was keen to make permanent. Davey had met producer Gus Dudgeon when working with Magna Carta, a folk oriented group who appeared to be making some headway when Davey left to take on session work. The extra edge he gave to the tracks and the obvious rapport he had with Nigel and Dee made it quite clear to everyone that Elton had the beginnings of a tight little rock and roll band. The heavy orchestrations of the first three albums were now a thing of the past.

'I was amazed you know when *Elton John* came out that we didn't get more haggled at for having an orchestra on it after *Empty Skies*. And although *Tumbleweed* did get more attacked on that score in fact there were only a couple of tracks — like *Burn Down The Mission* — where the orchestra came up on a large scale. Gus and I have already talked about the next album and we want to get back to a basic sound. I mean I'd love to do a Rod Stewart or Neil Young type of album — it's time for a change.

'Adding the new guitarist next year will give us

more scope I think. We've proved better than anyone that piano, bass and drums can make it in a loud rock act, but there's hardly any room for solos at the moment. I have to provide rhythm and solos on piano which is a bit of a drag and I think someone fresh in the group will take a bit of responsibility off me and give us a new lease of life.'

The antithesis of his live performances *Madman* was a somewhat dated mixture of brooding melody and obscure lyrics that the public seemed unwilling to unravel. The new mood was of instant catchy hits that demanded little of the listener and delivered their 'message' in the first twenty seconds.

Madman however was still firmly rooted in the late Sixties tradition. 'I'd say I've got rid of three years of shit. That might sound strong, but there were three years of songs and back catalogue which we've finally come to an end of . . . when we cut *Madman* . . . it was cut because we HAD to do an album, it was very painful. It was done under pressure and really tortured out of us, and I think it's remarkable that it turned out as well as it did.

'I still like that album, but really Bernie and I had hit a very odd situation when we came to cut it, we had written only about eight songs that year, working on them separately, and it came to the point that there was nothing to fall back on if we'd hated one of the tracks. Normally we write about 25 numbers a year so you can tell the sort of state we were in. So *Madman* wrapped up the tail end of our writing, and it was the very last album of its kind we'll ever do.

'Of course that doesn't necessarily mean we wouldn't work with Paul again. He's a genius and has something great inside him waiting to come out, but even he had a hard time on the last album because he had hit a crucial point in his own life and he had so much other work to get on with, like the *Macbeth* score. The one thing I'm a little upset about with Paul is that I don't think he's ever had the real recognition he deserves. Maybe he got some from our albums, but he never really got it when he worked on The Stones' tracks and on Nillson's *Without You.*'

Madman was a disjointed album, Taupin's lyrics nearly suffocating the moments of brilliance that John, Dudgeon and Buckmaster had contrived to create. One bright spot that still remains so today is the sensitive *Indian Sunset* which was written to highlight a problem both Elton and Bernie felt very strongly about. Elton: 'That song was a case of us really having something to say, and having to write a song to say it. The Indian situation in America really is appalling. If the American negroes are second class citizens then the Indians must be third class, they have the lowest life span and the highest suicide rate in the whole of America. They can't have jobs so they can't have money, they are doomed to live their miserable lives out on barbed wire encampments that the US government calls reservations.

'The Indian is the only history that America has, yet it wants to shut it up. The Indians legally own Alcatraz, but as the government wants it for an amusement park there's a running battle going on with the Indians shooting arrows at the customs boats, and scenes like that. They were completely cut off from the mainland until John Fogerty bought them a speedboat. A lot of kids in America want to do something about their plight, but there's nothing they can do. There wasn't much that we could do either. Political action would be useless, and anyway it's not really our scene, so instead we wrote a song.'

And Bernie added 'We write songs in strange ways. I write the lyrics first and just put a sheet of words on the piano for Reg. Then I go away and when I hear strange tinkling noises coming from the piano I know that there's a song on the way. I've come to the stage where I feel I've got to write about something before I can actually write it. I also have to be alone.

'We're not really the public's idea of a songwriting team. You know, two guys sweating over a hot piano, shirtsleeves rolled up, shades on. We're very unprofessional.'

As 1971 drew to a close Elton began to acquire the trappings of success. He bought a split level bungalow and stocked it with rare paintings and a large jukebox. He also invested a considerable amount of money in doing up the swimming pool and decorating the interior of the house to his own tastefully opulent preferences. He took the step of changing his name by deed poll from Reginald Kenneth Dwight to Elton Hercules John in an effort to shake off the stigma of his childhood unhappiness. He later stated that 'Hercules' was adopted in order to give him strength in times of self doubt. In February 1972, prior to journeying over to France to record the next album, Elton played the Royal Festival Hall in a concert that only went to highlight his current musical schizophrenia. For the first half of the show he performed the slower numbers with the Royal Philharmonic Orchestra under the baton of Paul Buckmaster and in the second half he ran through the rockers with Dee, Nigel and Davey.

The second part of the show was a rousing success but the first was later savaged by the critics. In the wake of several unsuccessful attempts by rock bands to perform with orchestras Elton's attempt seemed ill conceived and somewhat pompous.

The Band then left for France where recording began at the famed Chateau d'Herouville, a studio recommended to Elton by friend Bolan and Elton's tax conscious accountant! 'We made up our minds to do a group album with simple songs and very strong melodic lines. Bernie felt exactly the same, that there had been songs on past albums where I imagine people thought "what does he mean?" on certain lines. But these new songs are really direct.

'I don't think anyone realises the pressures artists go through when they record, putting their body and soul into it, and I can't explain the incredible difference it made working in France. We turned up with the studio booked and hardly anything else, and for two weeks it was like the Motown hit factory. Bernie was upstairs writing and Maxine (his wife) rushing down correcting his spelling, throwing the lyrics onto the piano and then me working on them with the band sitting around waiting to play as soon as I'd finished.

'Really everyone rose to new heights in France — especially with Davy in the band. It was the first time we'd really got together with him and he gave everyone such a boost. I don't think even Dee realised he could play bass the way he played on those sessions.'

And would this album mean an end to the accusations of Elton sounding the same with each consecutive release? 'To be honest I don't think I've ever become melodically constricted. I think maybe what people mean when they say things like that is that it's the construction of the songs — the fact that they might know the drums are going to come in at a certain point. But then don't most singers sound the same — in the sense that they're instantly recognisable?'

'Certainly I think this album will change their minds, but whether they stop criticising on another level — well I can't be certain about that. All I can say is that the whole business of recording this album has given us a new tenure of material, a real buzz.

'I think the whole band will get much more recognition from now on. It's no longer Elton John plus backing group. No, I would never have gone out totally on my own. There are times in America when I'll go on and do the first hour without anyone else. But I don't think you can carry the rock'n'roll thing on your own, it doesn't work. And emotionally I don't think I could have coped. I need other people around and I believe in sharing success. If you keep it to yourself you end up going stark staring mad.'

A single Rocket Man was released as a taster for the new album in April 1972. Bernie had come up with the lyrics on a late night drive in the countryside. They were one of only two sets of lyrics he had completed before setting off for the Chateau sessions. It had been a clear night and the stars glistened like diamonds.

To promote the single Elton and the band undertook another tour of the States. This time they included a visit to Houston's Manned Spacecraft Centre where he lunched with Apollo Fifteen astronaut Al Warden. The date of the visit also coincided with the 'splashdown' of Apollo 16 which of course made the single very topical and it was played to death on most of the country's radio stations becoming a major chart hit.

On 19 May 1972 the album was released. Honky Chateau was the turning point — a ten track tour de force containing three soon to be American hits and a host of other goodies. The mood was positive, the beat was strong and the brew was hot.

Honky Chateau was a success and Elton puts it down to it being 'more of an album you can relate to on stage. I knew they wouldn't be able to say "it's Elton John and his screechy orchestra". I hoped it would be the album to establish me in England. I'm always very paranoic in England — at Crystal Palace I was absolutely terrified.

'I'm not an "in" person to like, I know I'm not. It's all down to my records as to whether I sell. I've got a very loyal bunch of fans, but as far as the wavering masses go, it's up to the records.' With the success of the album came the hard round of interviews and press receptions.

'I've never minded doing them really but I'd got to the point where I thought I'd release Honky Chateau and see how it went. I haven't done interviews for a long time, basically because I haven't had anything to say. When the Madman album was released I did all the hype interviews, and it didn't do that well.

'Of course I was worried when it didn't sell well. When something like that happens, your ego is immediately deflated. I don't know what the main fault was, probably it was released at a time when people were sick of Elton John and Elton John records. I think we could have waited another six months before releasing it, but we had to release it then. There were reaons.'

'Madman marked the end of an era. It was the end of strings, and we got Davey in brand new. And by the time we'd got Davey, I was thinking of quitting. I thought I'd got as far as I could go.

'We had that important time in France — a time of getting to know Davey, because you can never be sure if someone is going to fit into a band or not. And as I was writing on electric piano, the band was happening. We were there for three weeks — no phone calls, no interruptions — that's the best way. Now, I know I could never get back to recording in three hour sessions.'

'Everyone involved with the album wanted Rocket Man released, but some others wanted different tracks. Still, we stuck to Rocket Man and I'm glad. I was proud of it because it's the best single I've ever released. In America someone thought the record was dedicated to the Apollo Missions. That's probably why we went to Houston and met the astronauts. Last May, I think it was — we just went over for three weeks, which I'm sure helped sales of the album. From now on I'm only going to make one tour of America a year. People get more excited if you only go once a year.'

The album went gold in America and no wonder. It was pure Americana but where Tumbleweed Connection had been country flavoured Honky Chateau was spiked with New Orleans 'jump piano' and hip swivelling funk. Exceptions were the two tracks Mellow and Amy, supposedly intended as tributes to the French musicians who played on the album.

Elton's Watford T-shirt peeks out between the bobbles

Rocket Man, with its plaintive verse and catchy chorus stood out, but it was only one of a very good crop of songs and that benefited from a fresh approach, functional production and the infusion of new blood. 'It seems like more of a group now that we have four members. There were restrictions as a trio. Our main problem was that the piano was the lead instrument, and, of course, it doesn't sustain notes — like Keith Emerson's organ does in ELP.

'But since Davey joined on guitar, it's been like a piece of cake for me. I can really relax when I play, whereas before we had to all work at filling in the sound.

'We went as far as we could as a trio and started boring the ass off everybody — including ourselves. Nigel Olsson remembers: 'There weren't any session men or gig orchestral arrangements or anything, we just went off to France and did it. Elton and Bernie wrote the stuff there, and after three days we were ready to go into the studio; we could record when we liked for as long as we liked, no hassles about booking sessions —

it's a good way to do an album that.

'It was all there. Bernie would write some words, bring them down to Elton, and an hour later, you'd have the song finished. It was unbelievable the way it was done.' Even while *Honky Chateau* was receiving unanimous critical acclaim in the press the band were thinking about the next album and rehearsing for a hectic three month tour of the States followed by visits to Australia and Japan.

'It's hard,' said Olsson, 'but I don't really worry about it because I'm doing something I really enjoy, and I know now that I'm really into music and stuff like that. Like looking back on playing with Spencer Davis, we had a good time, but I know I've improved 90 per cent since then, and I'm improving all the time.'

And Elton commented: 'Everything's changed since *Honky*. When we'd finished it in France Gus said it would be the album that would finally establish me in Britain. We all so desperately wanted it to succeed after the failure of *Madman*. We'd all decided not to have strings and we knew it was a good album but you can never be sure of anything working out the way you want it to. I think the album and the single was the major step for me this year, to re-establish me.'

4 GONNA BE TEENAGE

Through June and July of '72 the band were getting down to business at the Chateau, recording the next LP *Don't Shoot Me, I'm Only The Piano Player*. The title came from the old westerns Bernie used to see as a boy. *Daniel* was the first track to be recorded and it was intended as a tribute to one of Elton's closest friends. Although Elton dearly wanted it to be the next single, Dick James wanted two uptempo tracks to finally lay to rest the ghost of the quiet introverted singer/songwriter image.

The first single was *Honky Cat* from the still current LP while the fifties influenced *Crocodile Rock* was chosen from the new sessions and released two months later on 27 October 1972. 'I wanted it to be a record about all the things I grew up with like Bobby Vee for instance. I wanted it to sound like it does.

'Of course it's a rip off, it's completely derivative in every sense of the word. It's just something I've always wanted to do and after *Honky Cat* we could get away with it. If we'd released it after *Rocket Man* I think people would have been a bit shocked.

'I just wanted to release something different. And this gets me out of the old . . . well you know what I mean. It's just tongue in cheek, a bit like say *Speedy Gonzales*. Actually I met Bobby Vee in Los Angeles — it really freaked me out. Bobby Vee!'

Bernie took on a few of the chores to take some of the weight off his partner and to remind everyone that he was very much a part of the Elton John phenomenon. '*Honky* was very boppy, the next album will be very easy but very tight and hard. As far as the playing is concerned it's streets ahead of anything they've ever done before. I maintain, because it's partly my band, that at the end of the American tour it will be one of the tightest bands in the world. They're just so fucking good it's frightening.'

And he added 'Sometimes I think we've been the chopping block for every injustice, people say we were hyped. For God's sake, everything is hyped to a point, and anyway, what is hype? We didn't fly journalists anywhere in a jet.' A thinly disguised dig at the disastrous Brinsley Schwarz episode. Bernie felt very much a part of the music scene at the time, but fell shy of the growing infighting and politics of the music press.

'But wherever I look in papers I see Bolan challenging Bowie or Bowie challenging Bolan. Now that I do not approve of. I don't want to get caught in that syndrome; we never had that much done on us even at the beginning and I think they should cool it; I don't think we should get involved in this re-emergence of the glam rock bit.'

But Elton was keen to take the credit for his contribution to the showmanship in rock. '. . . whether you like it or not, we influenced a lot of people as far as dress goes. I look back now at some of the idiotic things I wore and wonder how I could have done it. Like that time in Boston when Maxine (Bernie's wife) persuaded me to appear in a long purple shirt and purple tights. But the thing I was getting at and trying to get across was "Here I am, a podgy little man in outrageous gear leaping at a piano". I don't want to sit there in Levis and T-shirt because everybody would go serious and say "Wow, great" and my songs aren't that serious, and so the answer to escape the James Taylor heavy syndrome was to dress up.

'I really wanted *Honky* to be different. I thought "right, no strings, we'll just use the band," and I got much more pleasure out of making that album than I did out of the others — it was a much happier album.

'And I love the Chateau — there's something about the place. For the new album, we went there with one song. Bernie was in America and posted me lyrics and I just sat down and wrote whatever I wanted. I really enjoy writing and recording, although I was in bad health, on the border of my crack-up.

'That Chateau is just very conductive to work. You just stay there for three weeks, you can't escape and drive up to London which you'd be tempted to do if you were doing it at the Manor or somewhere. There are no phone calls because the

A IDOL

(left to right) Nigel Olsson, 'Legs' Larry Smith, Elton, Davey Johnstone and Dee Murray at the London Palladium rehearsing for the Royal Variety Show, 1972

French phone system is so bad, so you're just in the middle of nowhere.'

The 'crack-up' Elton referred to had been brought on by overwork and had been building up for some time. As was usual in the rock business the only way off the treadmill was on doctor's orders. 'I went to America — to Malibu to rest — and when I got off the plane the first thing people said to me was "Hey, you're having a nervous breakdown" the news had got there that fast. I had glandular fever and was on the point of a crack-up; I was getting moody, shouting at people. I was never worried from a musical point of view but personality wise I was unbearable, that's the pressure of playing. I mean I've had exhaustion bouts but never a nervous crack-up like that.'

On recovering his health he found another tour of the States mapped out for the Autumn months beginning on 24 September. 'It's a big tour,' said Bernie, 'and it's going to be organised all the time rather like The Stones' tours. The promoter says Elton is the hottest touring property in existence at this time.'

'We've always had pretty organised tours,' mused Elton, 'but this time it will be our most successful tour as far as playing to big audiences goes. I love playing to 10,000 people at a time, and there's such a good energy level coming at you from an audience in the States.'

The American tour included two nights at the Los Angeles Forum where 'Legs' Larry Smith, ex-Bonzos, tap-danced in a Hussar costume complete with bridal train and two midgets in attendance! Later on 'Legs' and Elton danced to *Singing In The Rain* with a troup of leggy chorus girls and bucketfuls of glitter.

'You know me, I'm crazy. I had a vision of coming out and doing *Think I'm Going To Kill Myself* with Legs coming on wearing a crash helmet with a wedding couple on top, so I thought why not? You see, we've been doing a lot of outrageous things in America. One particular number we include is *Singing In The Rain* — Legs and I have a back track which the band recorded and we have a mock pianist in a complete tail suit and hunchback who throws glitter over us.'

During the tour he received an official invitation to appear at the Royal Variety Show in London. But the 'honour' was tempered with doubts. 'I knew about it before I went to America but wasn't allowed to tell anyone. But then I didn't really believe it — I never believe anything until I see it in writing.

'We finally got the letter in America, and I was still really surprised because I thought if they were going to choose anybody it was going to be

(above) Royal Variety Show rehearsals, 1972 (right) At Crystal Palace garden Party, July '71

someone like the New Seekers or Gilbert O'Sullivan. I suppose, though, I was an obvious candidate in a way — they would never choose a Slade or a T. Rex because they are not into that at all, which is sad.

'It's so boring, the sound will probably be dreadful. It's going to be chaos. It's chaos already. But I've never done anything like this before.' The show meant a break in the American tour which cost Elton about £15,000 in lost ticket sales so it didn't take much to provoke him. On returning to Britain he insensitively remarked: 'I'm here to do the show because 25 million people will be able to listen to my latest record and it will be the only chance I've got to plug it.' A hasty remark but one which he didn't seem to regret. Then it was back to the States leaving the publicity machine to make plans for the release of *Don't Shoot Me* in January.

'We made it under strain — I was very ill at the time. It won't be released till January because it would be lunacy to release two albums in five months. Like *Honky Chateau* it was recorded in

France — there will be some strings on it but the funk is still there. It's called *Don't Shoot Me, I'm Only The Piano Player* and definite tracks are *Crocodile Rock, Daniel, Teacher I Need You, Midnight Creeper, High Flying Bird, Texan Love Song, I'm Gonna Be A Teenage Idol, Have Mercy On The Criminal* and *Blues For My Baby And Me*.

'I'm sure singles do help an album. And I'm also sure you can afford to have two hit singles off an album. Singles now are getting much better, a lot more people are putting out maxi singles which is a good state to be in. But I won't neessarily be tied to releasing singles off albums — if I suddenly come out with a monster song I'd probably go in the studios and work it out.

'Yet at the same time I've now started to put out albums with singles on them. Bernie and I aren't writing so introvertly now. I'm also writing much more quickly. With the next album, Bernie sent me the songs from America — I went to France and recorded the whole thing. Then I phoned him up when it was finished and he flew in the next day to hear what we'd done.'

A month later he was still at pains to explain the change in musical direction. 'The American tour went very well. It was our first time playing really

big halls. We could have done it a year and a half ago, but we wanted to build up slowly. Anyway I don't think we could have played the big halls as a trio.

'We were really knackered at the end of the tour — mainly because we had to cancel some gigs in the middle to come back and do the Royal Variety farce. I thought I'd get bad publicity if I refused, but what an awful show. As a musical event it was the biggest non-event of all time — the most horrendous two-day stretch I've ever had.

'On the new one, there are only two tracks with the orchestra. Four of the tracks were first takes, and on one we thought it might be nice to have light strings — like on some of B.B. King's things. But it turned out heavier than that. The other track just needed something else — it's like *Imagine*, there are a couple of string things on that, but it didn't detract from the over-all album.

'I don't think we'll ever make an orchestra album again. I've gone off string players now. But I still think Paul Buckmaster is great.' One track *Teenage Idol* was about Marc Bolan. 'Yes, it's about Marc. "I sit cross-legged with my old guitar; going to get electric and put a silk shirt on." We played it to him, and he doesn't mind. It's just what he wants to be.'

Bolan and his wife June were regular visitors to Elton's luxury home in those days. In the year Marc was managed by June as a recording artist she often referred to their friendship with Elton, and his manager John Reid and she still sees them both. There is a great friendship between stars in the business, more so than you might expect. In a business where artists are constantly under pressure established stars can offer new ones the benefit of their experience.

'On an early Press release of mine I said that I detested pretentous groups like Tyrannosaurus Rex. Then I met Marc one day in a record shop and he sent me up about it. Marc comes down here quite a lot, I think he likes to come and relax. I didn't know what to send Marc for a Christmas present so I sent him that lifesize picture of me — the one with the dartboard for a head. Then, when it was my birthday, he outdid me — sent me a 27 ft. blow up of himself which came in a great big van, plus the silver disc for *Jeepster*.

'I'd always stick up for Marc — I like him. And Jagger is my idol.'

And now how did he meet Bowie? 'I heard Mott's single on the radio one morning and thought it was tremendous, so I phoned Bowie up and invited him for a meal. I'm still very star struck. I'm in the Bolan film — for about one minute. We recorded it down at Apple Studios. That was the first time I'd met Ringo. Ringo — I couldn't believe it. Jagger is my complete idol — if I ever met him I'd fall in a heap and die.

'I love The Stones, they are how a rock'n'roll band should be — loud, rude and vulgar. I suppose it's wrong to be so star struck, Marc tells me off about it. But that's just the way I am.'

Prior to the LP a new single, *Daniel* was relesed. The single had been put out against Dick James better judgement and only on the understanding that Elton would pay the publicity bills. Feeling strongly about the song Elton agreed and was proved right when it became another hit.

'It's a grower — *Daniel* isn't an instant single. But most people I played it to before it was released went away whistling it. Also, it's quite different from *Crocodile Rock*.

'There used to be a time when I did real slow singles, and I was bored with it all. I released *Honky Cat* just to get away from that syndrome. *Piano Player* has more fast things. We're more of a band now, instead of Elton John plus session guys. *Rocket Man* wasn't an easy single, and *Daniel* is exactly the same. It's one of the best things Bernie and I have ever written.

'For *Piano Player* I wrote the songs two days before the sessions — seven one day and five the next. I did the same thing on *Honky*. One day, though, I'll go to do this and nothing will come. We've got album-making down to a fine art now, so when we've got one coming out we'll just be finishing the next one. After *Madman* we caught up with ourselves. We stopped working and concentrated on recording.'

He was already planning yet another LP to be recorded when *Don't Shoot Me* was making its debut in the charts. 'The album comes out at the time I'm due in France to record another one. I haven't written any material for it at all yet — I'm going to leave that in the lap of the Gods.

'I didn't have anything worked out for the new one and it worked all right. As long as Bernie has got something I don't worry. If he hasn't we'll forget it — it will be an album like "Elton Plays George Gershwin".'

The album Elton described as his 'discoteque' LP was released to great critical acclaim on 26 January 1973. *Don't Shoot Me* was recorded when Elton was feeling 'down' but apart from *Daniel* the overall mood is one of four musicians totally involved and determined to have a good time.

He dubbed it a 'disposable' LP which was wrongly interpreted by critics to mean he was disappointed with it. Not so. '. . . *Don't Shoot Me* was a typical disposable album — it was a record for that few months that it came out, it bore a lot of

relevance to that time and I think people should just listen to it and enjoy it for that time and then put it aside and buy something else. There's so much stuff coming out that's good that you shouldn't say "I'm going to keep playing my *Don't Shoot Me* album and put everything else aside" because you're probably missing out on something else.

'I think that's what we mean by disposal. I mean take a normal pop record like a Strawbs record or a David Bowie or a Marc Bolan record, I mean they're perfectly disposable.'

As the LP raced up the charts (*Don't Shoot Me* sold more copies in three weeks than *Honky Chateau* had done in one year!) Elton revealed a hitherto secret ambition. 'It's really my ambition to do a completely introvert album — the kind of albums Jimmy Webb's been putting out recently, very honest, very personal. One day I'm going to sit down, maybe with Bernie and explain exactly what I want to do. I never want to split with Bernie but one day I'll just say well you've done your album — this one's going to be me.

'I don't want this to seem as though I don't enjoy what we're going now. I do, a hundred per cent. I really do get off on what I play. But there are two sides to every musician and there's definitely two sides to me — one has just never really come to the surface and I know I've got something in me that hasn't even started to come out yet.

'If I do that album I think it would surprise a lot of people . . . nobody really knows me — the person. But I know now that album would be quite a shock to the public because it would be a very, very doomy collection of songs.'

For his part Bernie was attempting inroads into production. He began by producing an album for songwriter David Ackles. 'Everybody should have a producer except Brian Wilson and he's my idol. David's material wasn't easy at the best of times, but he knows what he wants and he's a very intelligent guy. He just needed someone in the control room to level it all out. I loved doing it, it was very heavy and I'd like to work with something new that could unscrew me.'

Now an established and respected artist, Elton found himself the centre of many proposed business schemes. The germ of one began during the recent sessions in France. Guitarist Davey Johnstone wanted to make an album but Elton and his manager John Reid came up against a lot of problems when trying to find him a suitable record label.

'We got very drunk one night and said that we would just start our own record label' confessed a somewhat bewildered Elton. As the paperwork

Elton in 1977

piled up the directors assembled themselves and established their aims for the company.

'It's called the Rocket Record Company' declared Elton 'and we've started it already, although the first release won't be until January. There are five of us involved, myself and Gus Dudgeon, Steve Brown, John Reid and Bernie. I'd like something like Charisma Records, start off with unknowns and then build them up.

'I'd like to find an act I could produce — one I can concentrate on. And although at the moment I'm all idealistic about it, I realise it might fail. Still if I fail, at least I'll know I tried to make it better for some artists. I'm prepared to work hard too — I'll go in the office all day if necessary and hassle myself.'

And after the company signed Sunderland band Long Dancer (who included Olsson's brother) Elton stated the label's objectives and ideals.

'We just want to be a friendly record company, Rocket Records won't be like the Moody Blues' or Stones' labels, where the owners are the main act. First of all, I won't be with the label because I'm tied up with DJM. But I'd like it to be established by other acts. We've got about six cosy little offices in Wardour Street and we want to welcome all new talent.

'I know we'll attract a lot of freaks with that attitude, but it's the only way to make it work. Ideally we're trying to open a record company that's for the artist, both creatively and money-wise. I've poured all my money into this project because I really believe in it.

'We want to be completely open to any type of music. For instance, I really love The Stylistics, and if I could get a group like that I'd immediately drop everything and record them in America. I'm into a lot of black music and if I ever met a good reggae act I'd love to do that too. On the other hand, it'd be nice to find a nice young group with the energy of Slade.

49

'I'm appalled by the lack of knowledge of some people who have a lot of power in the music business. It really frustrated me. So as a reaction against it Rocket Records will offer people a decent deal with a good royalty rate.

'I got tired of being a puppet for people who aren't in it for the music — only the money from album sales. I know companies like Warner Brothers are nice people, but if you're nobody and your album is released the same week as 15 major artists, then you're not going to be the one to get the advertising.'

Recording plans were put aside while Elton gave full attention to his pet project. But his enthusiasm was tempered with a level headed business-like attitude. 'I've always wanted to have a record label, and the time is right now. It doesn't affect my relationship with DJM. I don't want it to turn into an Apple where we're feeding everyone. We're not going to try and release one sort of

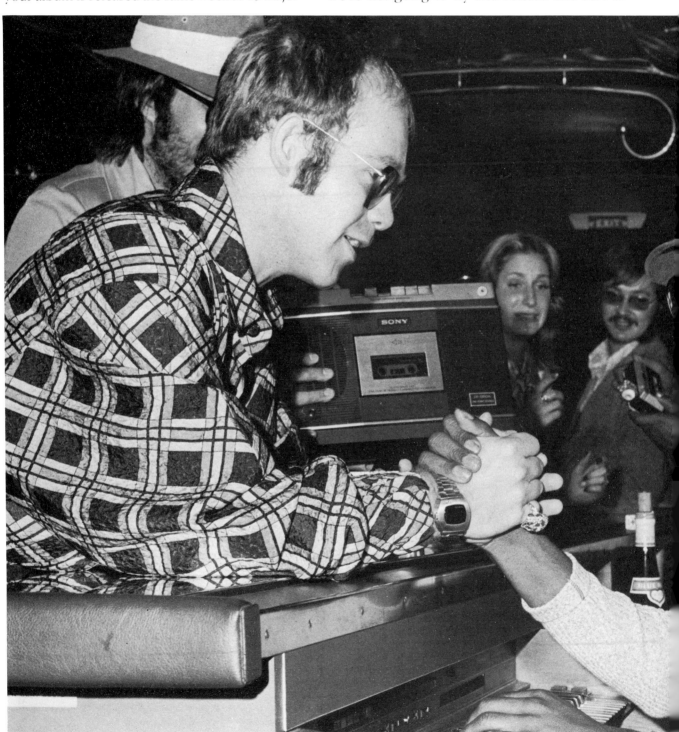

music; if someone came to me with a good reggae song I'd put in out.

'What we're offering is our undivided love and devotion; a fucking good royalty for the artist and a company that works its bollocks off. I'm prepared to sit in the office from dawn to midnight listening to tapes.'

But setting up a record company was not quite as easy as it had first seemed to be. A few months later they still hadn't released that promised

Johnstone album. 'The record company? Well, it's going all right, but it's just taking up so much time. It's taken us three months to find offices. But we've got our own logo sorted out.

'I don't think the label will be fully operational for about another six months. In the States my records are going out on Rocket/MCA — but a record company isn't something you can just invent overnight. Like, in the States, there's already a Rocket Publishing Company, so we've got to be known as the English D Rocket Publishing Company.

'Davy's Album is nearly finished and we've a couple of other people who we've nearly signed. But it's not fair to say who they are. Still, it's all coming along nicely.'

The label was finally launched on 25 March 1973 when a midnight birthday party was held aboard the sloop John D. Guests who toasted both Elton and his new company included Rod Stewart, Cat Stevens, Paul Simon and Ringo Starr.

Later on in May, Rocket chartered British Rail's 'Football Special' to ferry journalists to the official party in the very English village of Moreton-On-The-Marsh. The whole village turned out to witness the excesses of a music industry binge, as Elton, the band, and members of Long Dancer turned in a fine jam session. During the evening the guests consumed chicken, ham, salad, gallons of wine and one hundred and thirty-six bottles of champagne.

A couple of months later Rocket was introduced to America where Elton held a party on the Universal backlot. Journalists were flown in from London, Europe and other parts of the States to witness staged gunfights and another jam session between Elton, Nona Hendryx of Labelle and Sixties star Dusty Springfield.

By this time he was spending more and more on clothes, cars and specially made glasses — visibly enjoying his success to the full. For that 26th birthday party he had dyed his hair green and orange and announced he had just ordered the ultimate in optical flamboyance. A pair of specs that flashed E-L-T-O-N on and off, bringing the total of custom made glasses to twenty-four.

For the launch of the label in America he had worn white sports shorts with red piping, white socks, blue training shoes and a blue and green blazer covered in cigarette labels and topped with tricolour glasses — red, white and blue.

His recent shows had seen him take the stage in black and silver evening suit, red trousers, multi

Elton meets Stevie Wonder, 1973

(above) Elton with Bernie Taupin

coloured lurex socks and silver platform boots. 'I don't have them made, I have them built' he quipped. Guests at his house included the legendary Hollywood star Katherine Hepburn as well as John Lennon and Donovan. The house became the centre for Elton's extensive collection of stuffed animals and it was later necessary to transport some of the 'overspill' to his other properties in America. He bought friends and associates a myriad of expensive gifts including sports cars and a yacht for manager John Reid. Although the ludicrously extravagant jaunts and parties now too numerous to list, were undoubtedly the result of tax ploys as much as they were spur of the moment flings, there is no doubt that the gifts were anything other than unselfish gestures of gratitude. Elton has always been disarmingly generous though he claims that it stems from his fear that he may be knocked down one day and so he wants to enjoy life to the full at every opportunity.

Elton's collection of cars include several Rolls Royces, Daimlers, a Mercedes, a Mini G.T. and a vintage Bentley. His imposing assortment of antiques were chosen with a tastefulness the very antithesis of his garish preference in clothes. Some of his stage costumes were truly inspired. Designed and made up by one woman, Annie Reavy, they included a suit with a brick wall emblazoned on the front and above birds circling in a blue sky.

Another time consuming project was a piano cover in quilted pink satin with tiny bulbs that could be lit up and flash ELTON when required. A designer in Hollywood created red, blue and gold lamé suits with roses embroidered for Elton's off-stage use and, at one point, Elton had an all gold suit with gold bowler hat and green satin shirt.

The ludicrous clashes of colour and bizarre furry animal suits were so ridiculous that they made him endearing to audiences everywhere. His sense of fun and joy of performance were highlighted by them and far from detracting, they focussed attention on the music.

'I know I haven't the best image for rock'n'roll, and that probably gets in the way of my music sometimes. But most of my clothes are just for a laugh.' Plans were made to record the new album in Jamaica at the same studio that The Rolling Stones had been using. 'I always record outside this country, and I can't go back to the Chateau because of a legal hassle over who owns it.

'In Jamaica I hope to be cut off and uninterrupted. See, I like to stay where I'm recording, and it seems like the only place to go. Gus went to have a look at the studio and spoke to Charlie Watts, and

he says it's really conducive to hard work. Apparently, I'm not known out there, so that's really good.

'Gus had a long talk to Byron Lee and he said we'd have to go there to really appreciate the feel. Byron sounds a really great guy. We told him we like to play football machines and he's having one shipped over from Harrods. The only thing is, I haven't written any songs yet.'

The studio was booked on the assurance that the engineers would install similar equipment to that used in the Chateau. Elton made his way to the Carribean by way of a luxury liner. Using the ship's grand piano to write the material he had ammassed twenty songs in all by the time it docked in Jamaica.

Upon arrival at Dynamic Sounds studio Elton found a substandard piano and none of the promised equipment.

'At first everything was great — we rehearsed every single number so that in reality we could go on stage now and play twenty two new songs. Everyone was really up because we hadn't recorded for a long time.

'So we went into the studio, and first the piano didn't materialise and the Yamaha didn't sound right; then the mikes didn't arrive and we couldn't get any Dolbys. Ken (Scott) and Gus went into the studios for three days with Dee, Nigel and Davey to try to get a rhythm section sound but they couldn't get it together. So we had a meeting and decided to go home and count our losses.

'Jamaica was a harrowing experience — I'm not bitter about it, it's just one of those things that went wrong but I just wish they had got their things together because it could probably have been very good.

'As it's turned out the Chateau is back to normal again in fact better than ever under new management, so we're going to take a month out there.

'I did a radio interview on W.N.E.W. one of my favourite stations. I didn't really slag anyone off. I just said it hadn't worked out. We were going to do a tour of Germany in May which I was looking forward to but that's had to go by the board because the album's really important. We'll be recording for a solid month and in June we'll have to mix the album and overdub: I'm going on holiday in July as I always do, and in the first week of August come back and listen to the final mixes and authorise it, and then go on tour to the States. But it hasn't really mucked us up too much.

'We wrote one song called *Jamaica Jerk Off* which is sort of happy-go-lucky and a bit rude actually, so we're going to change it now because everyone'll think we're just having a go at Jamaica

Christmas Show at Hammersmith Odeon

so now we're going to call it *Jamaica Jerk*.

'We're doing one new number on stage — I don't want to make the mistake of going on stage and playing five new numbers because by the time you do record them you're probably sick of them so we're just going to an up-tempo thing called *Love Lies Bleeding*.

'The new stuff is so different — some of the things are going to be like *Abbey Road* and the tracks are going to interlace and I think there'll probably be quite a lot of orchestra. There's a Noel Coward type thing and. . .I've never had twenty songs together for ages and it's really going to be

nothing like *Don't Shoot Me* or *Honky* because although there are a lot of up-tempo songs, they're completely raucous, not in the vein of anything, not like *Midnight Creeper* which is a rock and roll song. I can't really describe it but it's going to be a double album and when Gus heard all the songs he decided we'd have to spend a lot of time of it.

'On the last tour of the States I did *Daniel* solo and we did *Have Mercy* and *Crocodile Rock*. But we've got so much material we don't know what to do: obviously we're going to drop things like *Country Comfort* and *Take Me To The Pilot* which I would have dropped years ago but people still ask for them. I still play *Your Song* and that's really the only old one I play. The band wanted to do *The King Must Die* again so we're going to do that again because we've never done it with Davey.'

(above) Elton with Kiki Dee

*(top right) Elton with his favourite football team
– Watford*

5 YELLOW

The year 1973 was a watershed year for Elton and Bernie. *Don't Shoot Me* had leapt straight in at Number One in the album charts, the autumn tour of America smashed all previous records set the The Stones and Elvis Presley and the year culminated in one of the classic rock albums of the Seventies *Goodbye Yellow Brick Road*.

Double albums are a dubious commodity in the music business, being either a collection of live tracks tracing a lengthy career or a single album's worth of material padded out with weaker songs to massage the artists ego. *Road* was neither of these. Four sides of glorious music, pertinent lyrics, perfectly orchestrated arrangements and sympathetic production without a single 'filler' on the entire album.

After the years of struggle and the erratic content of previous albums the various elements had finally come together in one magnificent package. Part of the album's success was that it crossed over into both AM and FM markets. Cuts such as the instrumental *Funeral For A Friend* which ran into *Love Lies Bleeding* and the Marilyn Monroe tribute *Candle In The Wind* were instant FM favourites. While the gutsy rocker *Saturday Night's Alright For Fighting* and the quieter, somewhat reflective title track vied for airplay on the AM stations Elton's immediate problem was to choose a single.

'I never thought *Crocodile Rock* would be a single though you never can tell until you get into the studio, but I've got about five songs that could be singles. There's one called *Candle In The Wind* which is a song about Marilyn Monroe and it's a real beautiful song. It's the only song I've ever written where I get goose bumps every time I play it. The only other songs I've ever written that affect me like that are *Daniel* and *Your Song*. There's also a song called *Your Sister Can't Twist But She Can Rock And Roll* which is a crib because it sounds like *Twist And Shout*, *Way Down Yonder In New Orleans* and it has the organ solo to *Palisades Park* but it really goes like the clap.

'Then there's a song called *Goodbye Yellow Brick Road* which is like one of the old Idle Race songs, but again there's so many — there's one called *Saturday Night's Alright For Fighting* which is so commercial it's ridiculous — *Jamaica Jerk Off* is so commercial but as I say you can never tell.

'*Rocket Man* I never considered as a single until we got in there. When we first rehearsed the numbers for *Honky Chateau* everyone said that *Salvation* would be the single, but when we got in there it didn't work out that way so you can't tell. One song that won't be a single is a thing called *All The Young Girls* which is about a lesbian. *Love Lies Bleeding* could be a single but I don't know anything about singles apart from *Daniel*.'

After further deliberation it was decided to release a total of three singles in fairly rapid succession. *Saturday Night* was the first followed by the title track and then *Candle In The Wind*. In the States public demand dictated the release of an unlikely track *Bennie And The Jets*. The demand for the track had been created when R & B station WJLB initiated an impromptu change of policy. The all black station chose Elton as the first white artist to be played and within three days it was top of their request lists.

The single was released in preference to Elton's choice of *Candle* and in addition to hitting the top of the American singles pile it also entered the R & B charts! The album went gold on the first week of release.

Prior to setting off for the most ambitious American tour so far E.J. took time to stand back and take a good long look at himself. 'It's fascinating actually. I've been throwing clothes out today and thinking "Did I wear that?" It's like high heeled shoes — I wouldn't wear anything else and I could never envisage the day that I didn't, but I think I'm not going to now.

'It's very strange that I've suddenly become fashionable and it's amazing, how, for example, James Taylor has become unfashionable after being very, very fashionable. I think Slade are going to become unfashionable — it's not their

BRICK ROAD

At Shepperton Studios rehearsing with China, 1977

fault it's just that people . . . there's always people coming up but it does you good to be fighting for your lives. I mean I wonder what's going to happen after all this glitter and camp?

'I never really took it seriously — it was always light-hearted and colourful. Obviously the people enjoy it and I enjoy it but I hope they don't really think it looks good. David Bowie's something else because he's got it all together and he really has got control over it and if you've got control it . . . it's like me I got to the stage where I didn't know what to wear on stage any more and now I think I'm going to start wearing evening dress because there's nothing to wear any more.'

The forty-two date U.S. tour began on 5 August and would culminate in spectacular shows at the Hollywood Bowl and Madison Square Garden. Beginning in Mobile, Alabama with an audience in excess of 12,000 the Elton John 'circus' rolled across the States playing extra shows to meet the demand and selling out massive arenas and stadiums including the famed Arrowhead Stadium in Kansas City which seated 28,000.

At the Hollywood Bowl Elton gave full vent to his love of both nostalgia and theatrical excess. A parade of bizarre look-a-likes strode onto the stage and each lifted the lid off the five brightly painted pianos collectively spelling out E-L-T-O-N as hundreds of white doves were released into the sky. The actors and actresses who bore uncanny resemblances to the Queen, Batman, Robin, The Beatles, Mae West and others then trouped off as Elton and the band took to the stage for a memorable set with all the trimmings.

The stage too had been decorated with plants and a neon staircase down which Elton entered resplendent in silver jumpsuit.

The after-the-gig party attracted a host of glittering Hollywood celebrities, none of whom had witnessed anything quite like this before. Shrugging off the worries of the reported twenty thousand bill for the cost of the show Elton bathed in the limelight shaking hands with the likes of Steve McQueen, Ali MacGraw, Britt Ekland and Carole King.

At the Madison Square Garden the stage show was toned down but the Walt Disney style costumes were not. Elton appeared in a silver lamé waistcoat, cavalier head-dress and a satin jacket. Even the piano had a pink velvet cover.

In October the tour reached Boston and to the delight of the audiences Elton found himself dueting with none other than Stevie Wonder. A frenetic performer, he took the audiences to the heights with sizzling rockets then eased them back down with the mellow *High Flying Bird*.

On his return to England Elton took the opportunity to rest, giving Bernie the chance to comment on reactions to the double LP. 'I think it's a major pinnacle as far as we're concerned' he began. 'A lot of people have said it's slightly the same as a concept album in the way that it flows, but I'm sure that's just the way the running order's put. I think it's the most important album we've put out but every album is an important album you have to keep establishing yourself. As soon as you let go your foothold you're going to go down, you can't scramble back up again'.

Too many people have tried to do that, a perfect example being Donovan. Of immediate concern was the follow up album and Bernie was naturally concerned that they should maintain the standard. 'I think it's even harder now due to the response we've had for the album. I'm sure that I knew people were going to like it as much as they did. I haven't really sat down and thought about trying to put something togther — I know that we'd basically like to do a concept album but finding the right approach for us because . . . it's easy enough for me to sit down and say I want to write a concept album but it's got to be much more of a joint effort than anything we've done before.

'I think that when I do get round to writing we will tend to do better than we've done before. It's like he's said before, he thinks his best stuff is still to come and that does for me too. So I'm not too worried about it, although I think what will be difficult about it is when it's presented on record — the overall sound of the whole thing because that's where we've got to change again. I mean we changed from the whole *Madman, Tumbleweed, Elton John* album stage, we changed to the looser approach of *Honky Chateau* and *Don't Shoot Me* and now we've combined everything into the *Goodbye Yellow Brick Road* album. And again now I think it's time for another change and that direction will come.'

Bernie viewed the progression on a parallel with his own maturity as a lyricist. 'I can write a slow song and I can write a rock 'n' roll song by just making it feel that way in lyric — I'm much more rhythmic in the way I put things down now whereas before when I was a lot younger I tried probably to make my stuff a little too arty-farty and try and make it not like a lyric because it didn't impress me looking at it. You have to makeup your mind whether you're going to write straight poetry or not and if you want to write lyrics to write very basically and make it rhyme and don't try and be clever.

'But that's the way I learnt because my earlier stuff is diabolical. I mean if you look at the stuff on

Another of EJ's fabulous outfits

the *Elton John* album it's so sterile, so cold, because it was written by somebody who was very young and rather naive. But I've now become a lot looser and the stuff I write now flows a lot easier.

'I don't believe that everything's been written and I don't believe it ever will be. I don't find it hard in that way because I don't write a lot of quote love-songs unquote because I find love-songs boring unless they've got an original twist to them, I just can't write those Bacharach type things, I'd much rather write on other subjects and if I do write something that's classed as a love-song I like it to have a twist to it like *I've Seen That Movie Too* using it in a different context.

'The perfect example of a straight love-song is *Your Song* but I could never write something like that anymore — I'd like to be able to but I don't think I could — it would just bore me because it wouldn't bear any relevance. 'Harmony' is a love-song but there's more subtleties to it, yet if you take that song and read the lyrics to it, it's really really banal but it's got a nice tune to it and the sentiments are quite nice . . . but I'm really a stickler for simple songs.'

At this time Rocket had its first taste of success with singer Kiki Dee. Kiki ws born Pauline Matthews in Bradford and she had spent much of her teens singing in the northern clubs. After unsuc-

cessful years with Phillips and then Motown she finally attracted the attention of Elton.

The single that became a hit *Amoureuse* had been written by the wife of Stephen Stills, Veronique Samson and had been translated from french by Gary Osborne. She had toured with Elton as backing vocalist to gain experience and everyone involved in Rocket felt she had the talent and only lacked the right guidance and back up.

Elton was a good mentor. He found her an excellent band comprising B.J. Cole and Jo Patridge on guitars, Mike Wedgewood on bass, Bias Boshell keyboards, and drummer Pete Clarke. He visualised her as the singer of raunchier numbers but saw a ready made hit in *Amoureuse*, the fourth single for the company.

It entered the Top Twenty soon after her appearance on *Top Of The Pops* and was followed by *Loving And Free* and the album of the same name. The album was produced by Elton and Clive Franks and included a couple of songs written by Elton and Bernie as well as four songs penned by Kiki herself.

In addition to writing for Kiki, Elton and Bernie wrote *Let Me Be Your Cat* for Rod Stewart. When it came to recording the track Elton was also roped in for piano and backing vocals. All in all it had been an amazing year; two Number One albums, the breakthrough of Rocket Records and it ended with a series of five Christmas concerts at Hammersmith Odeon and their fourth hit single of '73. *Step Into Christmas* was originally to have been a freebie, a gesture to the fans, but it developed into a legitimate release.

'It had been in our minds for a while, we were going to make a semi-joke single and give it away like the Beatles used to do but then Taupin said "why don't we make a good one" and spoilt everything.

'But the 'A' side really knocked me out more than anything I've ever done because it was so sudden I suppose but the 'B' side is very weird, more like The Mothers. The 'A' side is very Spectorish, it's like Darlene Love, I'm really pleased with it. I'm a sucker for Christmas singles and the fact that everyone else has Christmas singles coming out makes it more exciting — Slade have got one out, Wizard are bringing one out. But I just wanted to thank everybody very much for the year and Taupin came up with some beautiful lyrics.

'What have been the milestones of the year? Obviously *Goodbye Yellow Brick Road* because it's the best album I've ever done and it got such good critical acclaim especially in England. Also the record company has been a high-spot although at one point it was a low-spot and not functioning because we were too idealistic, but now it's exciting to watch someone like Kiki being successful.

'The Christmas single will be a high-spot — it's nice to go out with a hit and I think Kiki will have a hit and if we can have a hit with this Christmas song . . . It's been a really nice year for lots of things.'

For the British tour he planned to recruit a new member. Initially his thoughts were on the need for an additional keyboard player but by the time of the Christmas shows he had opted for multi percussionist Ray Cooper (formerly of Blue Mink).

'. . . We're getting closer to adding this new guy and that'll give us a lot if inspiration; if this person comes down and rehearses with us next week it'll be all over bar the shouting; he wants to join like anything it's just that he's very loyal to the group he's with. It'll change the sound because I want him to play keyboards; like when Stevie (Wonder) played with me on stage and when Gregg Allman

Side by Side: Elton (right) with his wax model at Madame Tussaud's

66

jammed on guitar you could tell the sound was much fuller.

'I still think we've a much better band than people sometimes give us credit for. There'll be a lot going out and we'll basically be doing some of the old hits and a lot of *Goodbye Yellow Brick Road*, much more than we did in the States. This tour we can really do what we like as long as we don't ignore some of the old ones, which people sometimes shout for.

'But in the States people want to hear different things — they shout for weird things like *Levon* and also *Amorina* and *Tiny Dancer* whereas here they want to hear *Rocket Man* so it's two different sets really, I mean I'd never play *Madman Across The Water* in England because it's not an English sort of song.

'I mean *Saturday Night's Alright For Fighting* is one of the best stage numbers I've ever written although people didn't accept it so much as a record. On *Yellow Brick Road* there are so many good stage numbers — like *Alice* is a good stage number, and *Grey Seal* and *Benny And The Jets* will be good stage numbers to do.'

The U.K. tour began at the Colstom Hall, came to Manchester at the end of November and climaxed at the Hammersmith Odeon. Elton's London Christmas shows are now an established part of the British Yuletide celebrations; a national institution. A Christmas without Elton would be like Christmas without turkey. The five Hammersmith shows had been sold out well in advance; everyone knew that these shows would surpass anything they had seen before.

The lengthy set began with an old favourite *Skyline Pigeon* played on a huge Steinway grand piano glittering in sequins. The band, now with Ray Cooper on a multitude of percussion, ran through all the hits plus a few classic album tracks such as *Funeral For A Friend*. The show ended with dry ice, an appearance by Her Majesty The Queen (hired look-a-like of course) and Elton in fine voice singing *White Christmas*.

For those who couldn't make the shows there was a rather superficial documentary made by Bryan Forbes which BBC television screened just before Christmas titled *Elton John and Bernie Taupin Say Goodbye Norma Jean, And Other Things*. It barely scratched at the surface in explaining one of the rock phenomena of the Seventies. A pretty vapid *Candid Camera* approach gave little insight into either partner's motivations, nor did it explain their attitude to the business in which they worked. The highlights of the programme were the songs sung by Elton alone at his piano.

6 DONT LE[T] GO DOWN

1974 was not a good year. It began with a rushed and disappointing album, *Caribou*, continued with a crisis and its only highlights were a *Greatest Hits* compilation, a brief teaming with John Lennon and a good business move (signing to MCA in the States for a record sum). Creatively though, '74 was a bad year for E.J. Like his fellow British stars who had enjoyed a surge of creativity in '72/'73, each feeding off the electric atmosphere, the muscle had turned to flab and the gutsy glam rock to marshmallow music. MOR ruled and rock had lost its way. After only twenty years it seemed to the cynical that rock had run its full course and, like many of its most innovative stars, had burnt itself out.

It was this stale atmosphere that led to the birth of the next hybrid — punk, two years later and to a re-assessment of themselves by the more astute performers. But at the time '74 produced such troughs as *Zinc Alloy* (Bolan's worst), *Smiler* (Rod Stewart's all time low), *Muscle of Love* (Alice Cooper's farewell to past glories), a whole host of dull and depressing produce and the emergency of such dubious delights as The Wombles, The Brotherhood of Man, The Bay City Rollers etc. etc.

Elton's contribution was *Caribou*, a loose and fairly unmemorable set that had obviously been fun to make but was not so hot to listen to. It appeared worse than it was due to the release only three months previously of the dazzling single *Candle In The Wind*, surely the pinnacle of Elton's career.

Caribou and the first single from it *Don't Let The Sun Go Down On Me* have not withstood the test of time too well. I remember seeing the marvellous singer/songwriter Randy Newman brilliantly mimicking Elton's songwriting and piano style and showing how basic it was.

After that Elton seemed to be doing the same, his songs fitted a formula and he became a caricature of himself. He is now firmly back in control but *Caribou* unfortunately remains proof of that period.

The album had been recorded at the Caribou

THE SUN ON ME

At a Tom Robinson Band benefit concert – Hammersmith Odeon, Xmas 1978

Studios in the Colorado mountains over a brief ten day period. It was mixed at the Record Plant in Los Angeles and released in June. As with previous albums, Elton had written, rehearsed and recorded in the studios, feeding off the energy and presence of the band. When the sessions were over everyone would unwind with jaunts in the ski-mobiles across the snowy mountain peaks returning to the secluded ranch for private film shows.

The LP opened strongly enough with *The Bitch Is Back*. Originally intended as the title cut, it featured brass from the Tower of Power horns, an uninhibited blast altogether. *Pinky* is an unremarkable little song about the winter at Caribou while — *Grimsby* is a sentimental journey back to Bernie's home town in a tongue-in-cheek Beach Boys style.

Dixie Lily, *You're So Static*, *I've Seen The Saucers* and *Stinker* are run of the mill E.J. tunes, better than most of the music being produced at the time but not on a par with his previous work. *Ticking* was Bernie's lyrical version of *Targets* (Boris Karloff's last film) in which a sniper terrorises a mid-western community.

Solar Prestige A Gammon is the ultimate filler, a nonsense song in English gobbledegook that makes *Don't Let The Sun Go Down On Me* sound like Elton's crowning glory. *Sun* was really a re-working of *Candle In The Wind* and *Daniel*, but his appeal was so universal by then that it became his biggest selling single to date! Despite his love-hate relationship with the song (he reputedly said 'I thought it was the worst vocal of all time') it was nominated for a Grammy Award for the best vocal performance that year. Indeed it *is* a fine performance and by anybody else's standard it is a damn good song but coming from the man who gave us *Candle In The Wind* and *Your Song* it pales by comparison. Critics seemed reluctant to praise the LP, calling it lukewarm and superficial. And Elton capped it all by saying 'I knew it would get slagged off, it seemed time for something of mine to get slagged . . . but it's just a period.'

Elton flanked by Sir Joseph Lockwood (left) and EMI chairman John Reed at EMI's 1976 sales conference

Producer Gus Dudgeon came straight to the point 'Caribou is a piece of crap' Gus and Elton had fallen out during the sessions, had argued for the first time over the content of their work and it left both somewhat bitter. The tension during the recording, the bad reception to the LP's release and the daunting schedule of touring finally led to Elton's most serious bout of ill health. A spring tour of Britain was cancelled and it leaked out that he was seriously considering a full retirement from the business. He emerged a thinner and healthier man after a couple of months total seclusion and rest and praised his manager and friends for pulling him through.

He claimed if he hadn't taken the band off the road when he did they would almost certainly have broken up. 'It was really becoming robotsville but the band is what I'm most proud of at the moment. I want things to happen as they come now, instead of plans . . . I'm the sort of person who'll say yes to things a year in advance, and then when it comes round I'll think "fuck, I don't wanna do that". I've been told that I've got to calm down on decisions, be told what to do for a change.'

Rocket was eating up a lot of money and taking up a disproportionate amount of time. The company underwent some pruning and founder director Steve Brown left. Several acts left the label, only Maldwyn Pope and Kiki Dee remained. Elton had been disappointed with the standard of material released and was contemplating a move to the label himself to bolster its image once his contractual obligations to DJM had been fulfilled.

'It's very hard running a record company,' he admitted 'I didn't realise it was going to be so hard. But I think the fault was just lack of communication between the five directors — me, Bernie, Gus Dudgeon, Steve Brown and John Reid — and I'm confident about it now. I think we've sorted it out.

'By the end of it all, we had hundreds of meetings, I was so cheesed off I just had to go away on my own, which is something I've never done before. I just pissed off to Arizona, couldn't take it. But now it's over, and I think it'll be all right." The long rest had restored his sense of reality, previously distorted by sleepless hours and lengthy periods of physical exertion without sufficient time for recuperation afterwards. He returned to the music business with a firm grip on reason, viewing whatever remained of his career as just a phase of his life and not his life's work; quite happy to take whatever would come to him day by day.

'Oh yes. I really would piss off, it wasn't fun. If it really became boring I'd say, OK, that's it. It's not worth it any more. A couple of times I've felt like that and we've had to change to make it a bit better.

A face in a (football) crowd

But honestly I'd really be happy to have my own record shop . . . my idea of happiness would be to stand behind the counter at a place like Tower Records in Los Angeles to see what people bought. I used to do it at Musicland when *Empty Sky* was out, and it fascinates me. I'd also like to have my own radio station so I could play some decent music.

'The thing I like about rock 'n' roll is that I don't have to take it seriously — I take it seriously enough but half the people you meet in America, for instance, take themselves far too seriously. I find that a pain in the arse. That's why I've always worn funny clothes on stage . . . it's been done in a humorous way because I couldn't compete with the Bowies or the Jaggers. I haven't got the figure for it. I'd look like Donald Dumpling from Dover, so I try to make people grin a bit. It's probably reacted against me a bit, but that's exactly the effect I wanted.

'Bette Midler said I should call my next album *Fat Reg from Pinner* which I thought was great.' Elton's admiration for other personalities was quite endearing. He enjoyed watching a professional at work, admiring their dedication and felt good in their company. He became a keen follower of the Wimbledon tennis tournament where he met champion Billie Jean King. It was the start of a long and happy friendship.

'I met Billie Jean King in 1973 and she invited me up to the players' box every day at Wimbledon. I even managed to get a game with her husband on the Wimbledon practise courts.' He developed a keen interest in the sport and even spent a month at a training centre in the States.

'That started off my weight loss. The mid-day temperature out there on that ranch was about 112 degrees. Since then I've lost about two stone in weight.'

He also had a brief flirtation with cricket which ended abruptly after he turned up for a friendly match at cricket's hallowed ground, Lords, with his hair dyed a bright shade of green!

'I don't socialise with people in the business really — the only person I know really is Rod. I socialise more at Watford Football Club than I do in the music business. Things like meeting Billie Jean King . . . I suppose I'm a bit like Alice Cooper in that way — any chance I get to meet someone I really admire I take.

'I think it's always good to have idols, people you respect, and I've got more sporting heroes than anything else. I think you need to be a special kind of person to be a top sportsman . . . anyone can be a rock star, "Wanna make a record?" There's a lot more dedication in being a tennis champion

or something than being a rock musician — like I'm sure The Rolling Stones don't get up every morning and have a band rehearsal. Rock 'n' Roll is far more loose, far more fun, but I can't imagine a bigger thrill than scoring a goal in the World Cup or something.'

Elton's love of football began when, as a schoolboy living 'round the corner' in Northwood, he would see local team Watford play each Saturday afternoon. Until the mid-Seventies football was unrivalled as the national pastime until a combination of hooliganism and rising ticket prices drove people away. The 'never had it so good' generation found themselves forced into making economies and entertainment was the first luxury to go.

Rock stars offered better value for money and they guaranteed a good time, especially showmen like Elton. He however remained loyal to his boyhood team, eventually becoming vice-president for the sum of fifty-three pounds, but he knew it wasn't enough. Football was in big trouble and a fourth division team like Watford could easily go under. Elton's patronage was viewed initially as a publicity exercise but subsequent events have proved that untrue.

A charity concert in aid of the ailing club was one of only two shows he played in May after recovering from his recent illness. The other was for the Invalid Childrens Society, honouring a promise to a lady who has since become a dear friend, Princess Margaret.

The former event was to be held on 5 May at Watford's own ground, where 30,000 were expected to turn out to see him; the latter at the Royal Festival Hall where Elton planned to run through his hits in chronological order

Prior to the Watford benefit he announced a further development in his commitment to the club. He became a director and promised financial aid as well as moral support. 'Our gates are up 3.4 per cent this season' he announced proudly, before speculating on the forthcoming show. 'We're hoping for about 35,000 fans. Surprisingly there hasn't been much opposition at all from the local authority. Everybody has been very helpful although we were a bit worried about the hospital which is next to the ground. Apparently the geriatric ward directly faces us but we had a meeting about it and some guy said not to worry because most of them were dead anyway!

'The only one I've attempted like this was at Crystal Palace which I regarded as a bit of a disaster and knowing my luck it'll turn out pouring with rain and about three people will turn up.

Elton at home in England, 1982

(above) Relaxing at home watching tv, 1982

(right) with Kiki Dee, 1974

'I suppose the next one I'll do for Watford will be in aid of the chairman's pension fund. At the moment we're negotiating for another top British band to appear with us and the concert will also give the fans an opportunity to hear our new material for the next album. The Festival Hall gig though will be entirely different. It'll be something like the history of Elton John and we'll go through from beginning to end, sorry, to where we are now.'

And that slip of the tongue added speculation to the rumours of a scaling down of all public appearances and an end to the massive tour schedules. 'For a start I promised that I'd do these two shows anyway — the decision to cancel the tour was taken in New Zealand and it was an automatic choice.

'It was a decision to either break up or rest for six months, we were becoming like robots on the road and the band haven't really had a rest in three or four years — they have got wives and children ya know.'

It was obvious that he was taking his job at Watford seriously; it wasn't just another rock star on a patronising ego trip. He even persuaded fellow football fanatic Rod Stewart to join him and the team in training. Considering his weight problem Elton John has always been a very active man.

Elton entered the record books on 13 June 1974 when he re-signed to MCA records in the States, which guaranteed him a twenty-eight per cent royalty and eight million pounds in advances over a five year period. The company were desperate to keep the superstar both for financial reasons and to keep a figurehead and identity for the company. President of MCA, Mike Maitland, was spared a really tough fight as John Reid was already half-convinced in his own mind against switching labels just for the sake of a change. Reid knew that if he took Elton elsewhere (Elektra-Asylum seemed the most likely at the time) then it might take him two years to establish a good working relationship with the company's personnel, by which time his artist may have gone under.

In August another track was lifted from *Caribou* and released as a single. *The Bitch Is Back* romped into the charts care of a great hook and machine-

gun riff from Davey Johnstone. Elton had no intention of putting all his efforts into the fickle rock 'n' roll business. Not content with an active role in the career of Watford, he took his first step into the world of movies with Ken Russell's film version of Pete Townsend's rock opera *Tommy*. Elton had previously made a don't blink or you'll miss me' appearance in friend Bolan's unsatisfying *Born to Boogie*.

He played piano on one or two of the songs recorded at Apple studios with Ringo Starr on drums and seemed bemused by Bolan's ego flexing throughout.

When it came to *Tommy* however, the presence of Russell and the promise of a really good part persuaded him to have another try. Elton had apparently told his friend Rod Stewart to turn down the part when he was offered it because, Elton explained, he would be stuck with the image of the 'Pinball Wizard' having sung the part on Lou Reisners LP. When Elton turned up in the movie playing the part he had told Rod to turn down, Rod was none too happy!

Balancing on stilts five feet off the ground and walking in huge bovver boots, Elton attacked the role with gusto and made it a great success. He only appeared in one short four minute segment but along with Tina Turners *Acid Queen* his is the cameo highlight of the movie. In interviews he mentioned the role only in passing. 'I just finished doing the Pinball Wizard part in the *Tommy* film. It only took three days and I was just photographed doing mime to the music. I think it'll be a great film and am really looking forward to seeing the completed version.'

Meanwhile *Caribou* had fared better with the public than at the hands of the critics, reaching platinum status in America. E.J. and entourage returned to the ranch in the summer for another round of sessions which would form the basis of the 1975 LP *Captain Fantastic And The Brown Dirt Cowboy*. This time Bernie had written his lyrics prior to the sessions though Elton, as usual, left his side of the partnership until the last minute. He used the grand piano on board the *SS France* as the ship made its way across the Atlantic.

While in the States he visited John Lennon whom he had met briefly the previous year and was then invited to guest on Lennon's *Walls And Bridges* album. In return the ex-Beatle stopped off at Caribou to play guitar on Elton's version of *Lucy In The Sky With Diamonds*.

'I met John last year; and then when I was in New York after getting off *SS France*. I saw him again and he said, "come down to my sessions." So I did, and ended up doing, *Whatever Gets You Through The Night*, and *Surprise* from the album. And he was going to L.A. to do a song which he had written for Ringo, and I said: "On the way back, why don't you come up to Caribou? Cos we're gonna do, *Lucy In The Sky*" and he said "sure".'

A promise was made during those sessions that if Elton's *Lucy* single made it to number one then Lennon would have to appear on stage with Elton during the forthcoming tour. In haste Lennon agreed and thought no more about it.

The American tour began in October and would take, in forty four cities, with Kiki Dee and her band as support on each date. The audiences totalled three quarters of a million and five million dollars swept in at the box-office. His shows were the places for Hollywood's faces to be seen and at the L.A. forum he saw Elizabeth Taylor, Barbra Streisand and Diana Ross amongst the audience.

'In February, I felt that I never again wanted to go back on the road. But after my rest, I just want to get out there and play to the fans. We usually do one tour of America a year. However, after working on the road for a period of over four and a half years we decided to take time off and relax. We haven't really toured anywhere since February and it's been six months since we've done anything at all.

'It's very strange . . . I've toured America so many times and never really had any screamers until now. In England, you take your life in your hands when you go on stage . . . they scream for almost anybody. Over here it's rather funny, really, especially me . . . I can see if I were Mick Jagger or someone like that. I find it very weird, I suppose it's a new generation of rockers.'

For Kiki Dee this was a major step in her career; a never to be repeated opportunity. 'I'm more than pleased. Having known Elton for a while back home, I feel very at ease. The whole Rocket organisation has been just great, giving me the freedom to do just what I like. I was restricted with Motown, but the feeling now is tremendous.

'I try not to think of myself as a girl too much when I perform. I feel it's a dangerous thing. The most important part about trying to be a performer is to just think of oneself as a person. I think I've been pretty successful at that.

'I've just come off a six week tour with The Guess Who, Steely Dan, and The Beach Boys. I've already done a tour with Elton in England.'

The addition of a brass section gave Elton's band extra bite while Ray Cooper's command of percussion and his own extrovert antics added a welcome dimension to a familar number like *Levon*.

Meanwhile time was ripe for a 'greatest hits' collection and Elton was drawing up a short list of tracks between gigs. 'MCA wanted to put out a greatest hits album. It sort of gives us leeway and a chance to rest for we won't have to come up with anything new. It gives us breathing space. However, we have done a new album that'll be released in May.'

'It'll be titled *Captain Fantastic And The Brown Dirt Cowboy*. It's a story type album about Bernie and I. But it's far from a concept work.' When asked about his retirement plans (!) he confided 'I think I'll be a football club chairman in England. I just did a successful benefit with Rod Stewrt for the soccer field in Soho. We got 40,000 people there and raised a lot of money. That's where my heart lies. I never really thought I'd be a rock star. I just wanted to write songs and never ever tour after I was with a group for five years . . . But it just didn't work out that way.

'I'm having a great time. Too many artists don't have a good time, and that's bad.'

Midway through the tour, on 8 November *Elton's Greatest Hits* was released, featuring nine hit singles and just one LP track *Border Song*. So strong was it that in the first week of release it was Number One in the U.K. taking only one week more to achieve that honour in the States! Elton, in a characteristic show of modesty, attributed its success to its 'pretty strong' track listing.

By the new year it had gone platinum, a rare achievement for a collection of old tracks. During his stay in the States he still managed to keep an eye on Watford. 'When I'm in America, I ring Watford football club every Saturday when the game is either going on or is over, to see how they're getting on. When I'm home, I go to every match.

'I owe a great deal to Watford. They gave me a sense of balance. They were the sanity to the pop side of it all. They say they owe a lot to me. But I owe far more.' On 15 November *Lucy In The Sky With Diamonds* was issued, coupled with another Lennon song *One Day At A Time*. At nearly six minutes in length DJ's seemed reluctant at first to give it so much needle time, but it was such a good cut that it was soon top of the playlists.

At Elton's Madison Square Garden apearance in New York on Thanksgiving night (28 November) John Lennon strode on stage for the first time in years and duetted with Elton on *Whatever Gets You Through The Night*. The crowd couldn't believe their eyes or ears and remained stupified through *Lucy In The Sky With Diamonds*.

Lennon then made an announcement. 'We were trying to think of a number to get me offstage so I can be sick. We came up with this one — written by an old fiancé of mine called Paul.' There followed a truly great version of *I Saw Her Standing There* — the first track on the first Beatles album and one for which Lennon had not previously sung lead.

It had been Elton's idea to do that song after Lennon rejected the familiar *Imagine*. The atmosphere was highly charged and Elton admitted to shedding a few tears. 'The rush I felt came from the audience . . . it was magic.'

This was the peak of his success, the albums went to Number One, the stars swarmed around to bathe in his limelight and when the tour finished in December it was said to have grossed over six and a half million dollars. Elton's *Greatest Hits* stayed at the top of the pile for a staggering ten weeks in America and became MCA's fastest selling album in the history of the company.

On his return to Britain he renewed his interest in Watford F.C. and began to spend the fruits of his labours. 'Hercules' (his Surrey mansion) was fast becoming cramped with the expensive souvenirs, collected the way some people gather shells on a day trip to the seaside.

'I'm buying a lot of art deco furniture from auctions. They are prize pieces, mainly from museums and are very expensive. It upsets me a bit that I can't actually go and bid for them myself, but if I appear at Sotheby's, it immediately puts the price up, I'm told.

'I know I'm one of the highest paid entertainers in the world but I honestly didn't go into it for that reason. I suppose I could throw it all up tomorrow and have enough money to live on for the rest of my life. But I just couldn't do it. Besides, I've still got lots of ambitions. That's the whole fun of it. There wouldn't be any fun if there weren't any ambitions left. Each year I think it can't possibly get better, and there is always something which comes up to try for.'

Elton's mother and stepfather moved in with him around this time and to make room he removed a priceless collection of paintings into the garage! His collection of custom made glasses became so large he kept them in specially designed cases and during one tour he had them transported in a special car of their own.

'It's a flair for the ridiculous that started me off collecting crazy glasses.' But there was nothing ridiculous in his claim to be a multi millionaire. His 'accessories' took the form of diamonds which spent much of their time in vaults at Cartiers. He thought nothing of buying a £3,000 Fabergé clock and giving it to John Reid as a 'thank you' present in

With Kiki Dee and his mum

1975 together with a £25,000 yatch.

The two acre base in Virginia Water creaked with the valuable horde, and so after a visit to John Lennon's expansive private estate he snapped up a £400,000 house in Berkshire. The 'garden' spread out over 37 acres and included a riding stable, vineyard, and, of course, a tennis court. The house had a private cinema, six bedrooms and six bathrooms.

The following year he spent one million dollars on a house in Los Angeles previously owned by John Gilbert, Greta Garbo and David O. Selznick. By February '76 however he had decided to economise and put his Surrey house up for sale at £125,000.

When travelling on a shopping expedition he would use a private jet with a Cadillac or Rolls Royce to ferry him to or from the plane. One such spree saw him arrive at Cartiers with an extensive shopping list. Half an hour later he left with £3,000 worth of gifts for the staff at Rocket; a gold cigarette lighter, a necklace, a set of suitcases and assorted jewellery.

Before boarding the jet and returning home he whipped into an exclusive gallery and spent a further £1,500 on sculptures and elegant 'dust-traps'. With an estimated net income of £3 million a year it was also in his own interests to spend extravagantly to avoid the crippling British tax bill. Beneficiaries of this rare affliction included a secretary who 'bagged' a £1,200 raccoon coat, a business associate who drove away a brand new Rolls Royce and Rod Stewart who qualified merely by reaching the ripe old age of 30. Rod's birthday present was Rembrandt's etching *The Adoration Of The Shepherds*. It was only one of several Rembrandts and Magrittes that Elton owned.

Being in the top income bracket meant that he was forced to pay 83% tax. Despite being strongly advised to the contrary he decided to stay in his beloved England even if it meant he had to 'pay through the nose' to do so. It was at this time he professed 'I can see the day coming when I will stop playing music and make helping Watford a full time job.' That day wasn't as far away as he thought.

CAPTAIN

Sitting on the tapes for *Captain Fantastic* waiting for the right moment for release was a necessary aggravation. Elton was used to hyper-activity but realised that to release a new album while the old one was still in the charts was a bad move. So he took Reid's advice as usual and waited.

One day he received a call from Neil Sedaka inviting him over to the star's London apartment. Sedaka had been a huge star in the early Sixties — in a way Elton's equivalent of the time. Both write bouncy piano based songs, enjoyed a universal appeal, were unlikely heroes and were top class showmen. Sedaka, an American, had returned to Britain in '73. He was now enjoying a revival in his career at least in the UK, but it emerged that he had not secured a contract in America.

What began as a friendship developed as Elton signed Neil to Rocket for the American territories.

The ideals of Rocket were once again in action; a close relationship first and a hard push for the product to follow. With both Kiki and Neil it was easy to see that the 'family atmosphere' envisaged at the formation of the company was now a reality. Neil's career was given an added boost when his new mentor guested on the single *Bad Blood*.

'Well, just now I seem to be the world's top paid session singer, but no-one ever asked me before! Usually they think: we won't have him on it, boring old fart! I only appear on people's records that I know. I'm just beginning to enjoy myself and loosen up a bit.'

The song became a Number One in the U.S. and Elton was as pleased for Neil as he would be for any of his successes. To end '74 on a triumphant note Kiki Dee had another hit for Rocket with *I've Got The Music In Me*. The year that had nearly split the band and saw Elton take a premature retirement had at least been tempered by an amazingly successful U.S. tour and a good year for his pet projects Watford F.C. and Rocket Records.

Caribou however remains a disappointing work, though it too would be superceded by a splendid album, the autobiographical *Captain Fantastic And The Brown Dirt Cowboy.*

On 28 February 1975 the single *Philadelphia Freedom* was released, backed by the live version of *I Saw Her Standing There* with John Lennon. The A-side was written for tennis friend Billie Jean King who was delighted with the song which shot to Number One in the States as if by birthright.

Someone Saved My Life Tonight followed ten weeks later with the album just days after that. 'I think this is the best album I've done. Better than *Yellow Brick Road*, and I was very pleased with that one. It went well from the start and song-writing was no problem. I defy anyone to say it sounds like me, because it doesn't. I can't think where this new voice has come from, but it's most peculiar. It's the first concept album we've done and it's about us, how we started and what it was like.'

One of the tracks *Bitter Fingers* harked back to the time he played piano in the Northwood Hills Tavern. 'That was the best training I ever had. Now you really have to keep your wits about you for that job.' He described the 'concept' as 'Just experi-

FANTASTIC

ences of Bernie and I, how we got together through the advertisement, and all our experience up to the *Empty Sky* album . . . we just set it around the idea of our disappointments and things. It's really not a concept album. There's a few personal songs in there as well. It's the first time we've written an album where Bernie has had the running order for the songs before I wrote the melodies. That was very strange; but it's worked out well.

"I sometimes think if it all ended tomorrow, I'd like to work in a record shop – or open my own."

(pages 82 & 83) Elton always favours picturesque travelling clothes

'Caribou was made in like ten days, whereas this time we really cooled it and had three or four months off, cancelled the English and European tours because we were exhausted. And when we went over to Caribou this time we booked five weeks studio time which we've never had the luxury of doing before. Also with *Caribou* there were a few personality problems; everyone was shouting at each other because we were tired. I still like the album. I prefer it to *Don't Shoot Me*, but there you go.'

Captain Fantastic together with *Greatest Hits* and *Yellow Brick Road* make up the cream of Elton and Bernie's work. Despite lukewarm reviews on its release *Captain Fantastic* still sounds good today. *Someone Saved My Life Tonight* is the harrowing story of Elton's suicide bid that turned to black comedy when he turned the gas on but left the windows open. It was a painful experience to have to relive and during the recording of that track Elton was repeatedly shaken by the memories, almost to tears, as Gus Dudgeon unwittingly led him through it again and again to perfect the vocal track.

It is an unhappy album tinged with bouts of self pity and frustration. Perhaps this was the LP he had sometimes talked of making, the introverted album that would 'surprise everyone' because it was so 'down'. On the record he was admitting to unenviable traits in his own character; professional jealousies and the like, putting himself 'on the line' like never before. Taupin's lyrics were devoid of pretention because they spoke of the partners' shared struggles and Elton's reflective music became the voice for his own very personal pain.

It was an intimate album and one in which you share the joys and frustrations of its creators. Elton's voice is controlled — he has been accused before of treating the lyrics as throwaway lines, but on tracks like *Better Off Dead* and of course *Someone Saved My Life Tonight* he is more assured, trying as hard as he can to put across what are very personal hopes and fears.

Bernie's description of his partner is admirably perceptive, though he tends to over romanticise what must have been a pretty squalid existence as the pair submerged their own talents beneath a welter of conveyor belt Tin Pan Alley dross. Elton admitted that watching others make the grade while he and Bernie had struggled made him resentful but even more determined to succeed. The songs on the album, with the exception of the lightweight *Tell Me When The Whistle Blows*, have the tension underlined by a bittersweet melody line.

For Elton though it was a full stop in his career; time for a change. The decision to change the band was a hard one. A successful partnership is usually dragged kicking and screaming to a slow death in the music business. Lawyers, managers, agents and record companies cajole and persuade the partners to drain their creative juices dry before letting them leave, but for Elton it seemed Bernie was the *only* partner.

He was looking for a new sound that Nigel and Dee couldn't provide him with. Both were told of the news by Elton who couldn't adequately explain that he just needed a different approach and that their dismissal was a hard decision for him to make but a most necessary one.

Five years had been a long time to stick with the same line up but he felt they had gone as far as they could together. Nigel and Dee were naturally shaken by what appeared to them to be a sudden decision and despite attempts by Elton to keep their friendship they drifted apart from Elton, admitting that they were both 'hurt' by it all.

Elton John and Bernie Taupin were always open to suggestions from the people they worked with and so it is only fair to point out the contribution that Nigel and Dee made to the records on which they played. When the new band produced *Rock Of The Westies* the following year it was still Elton and Bernie up front but the sound of the music had changed. In rock sometimes the sound is as important as the music. When Nigel and Dee left things were never quite the same again. The new band consisted of Kenny Passarelli (fretless bass and backing vocals), James Newton-Howard (keyboards), Roger Pope (drums) and Elton's old friend Caleb Quaye on rhythm guitar.

Caleb had met Elton when both were tea boys in Tin Pan Alley and he later joined Bluesology. He was earning a good living as a much-in-demand session guitarist in Chicago when he received a call from Elton offering him the job of second guitarist. Roger Pope had been roped in for the *Empty Sky* sessions by Caleb and he had also played on *Tumbleweed Connection* and *Madman Across The Water*.

After that he lost touch with Elton until a phone call summoned him to a series of rehearsals in Amsterdam. He had also been the drummer for Kiki Dee during the summer tour of the States. James Newton-Howard was a last minute replacement for a keyboardist who turned down the lucrative offer but as if by fate he was the most obvious choice. Passarelli had played with Stephen Stills and Joe Walsh. It was Walsh that had recommended him to Elton.

The new band was premiered at Wembley Stadium on Midsummers Day 1975. The one day festival attracted the legendary Beach Boys, The Eagles and Joe Walsh, all would share the bill equally with Elton and each was allocated a ninety minute set. Elton was now used to sets of up to four hours but with a new band and a new album to 'run in' the time was more than adequate. The event was witnessed by 120,000 fans but for once the shared bill was not a success. The crowd had to wait all day to see Elton who included only a handful of familar numbers and battled against a less than adequate sound balance.

The biggest mistake was in performing the whole of *Captain Fantastic* to an audience unfamiliar with the album. The Beach Boys came off the best sticking to their tried and tested oldies. Elton shrugged off the bad reviews and left soon

An early Rocket publicity shot

after to begin work on a new LP at Caribou.

Rock Of The Westies was a happy if flawed LP. The intention had been to ease the new musicians in through an 'uptempo' collection of tracks where spirit would take precedence over everything else. It may have been fun to make but as a follow up to *Captain Fantastic* it palled by comparison.

Elton later admitted that the songs 'may not be the greatest I've ever written'. Originally the title of the album was to have been *Bottled And Brained* and the single scheduled for release was *Dan Dare*. By September title and single were changed with *Island Girl* shooting up to Number One in the States, care of Ray Cooper's Caribbean percussion treatment. The album followed likewise; only the second LP to hit the top slot in the first week of release. Elton had already taken the first honour with *Captain Fantastic*!

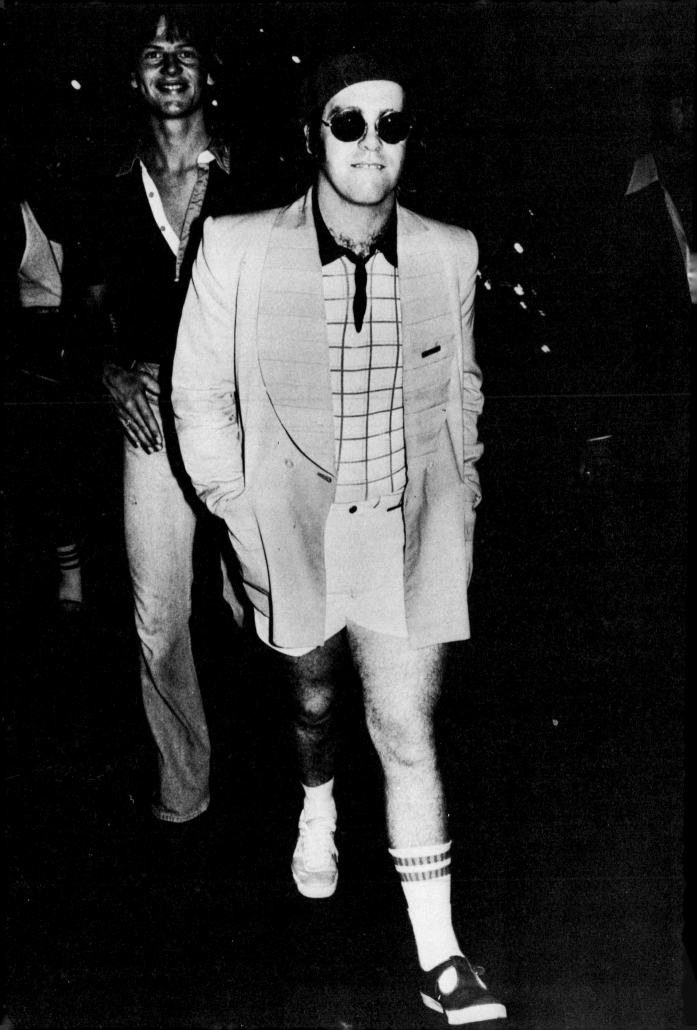

Sadly *Island Girl* was the only track strong enough to be lifted as a single but in terms of sales figures and as a concert attraction Elton had no equal. He was the undisputed superstar of the Seventies.

A short tour of America's West Coast followed which included two nights at the Dodger Stadium in Los Angeles. The stadium had been used just once before for a rock concert and that was when The Beatles played there in 1966. It is a indication of E.J.'s status in the States that he was singled out for this particular laurel. Elton himself was given a more lasting honour two days before the Dodger shows when he stepped into history by unveiling his star on Hollywood Boulevard's Walk of Fame.

Elton John was now literally next to Marilyn Monroe, Judy Garland and all the other legendary stars and his place in show business history assured. His only words during the ceremony were typically off-hand 'I declare this supermarket open' he quipped and have an acknowledging wave to the 5,000 strong crowd held back by a police cordon.

The Dodger Stadium — 23 October and 24 October 1975. They were the days that saw the peak of Elton's career. 55,000 attended each performance, bathed in sunlight and wallowing in four hours of glorious music. Never again would he see adulation on such a scale. He had sold fifty million albums and broken box-office records around the world but after the tour he would again comtemplate retirement.

The *West Of The Rockies* tour had netted two million dollars in ticket sales but had taken its toll on Elton's health. Doctors prescribed four months complete rest which he gladly took in the island paradise of Barbados. He maintained a low profile for most of '76 and his popularity waned as a result. *Grow Some Funk Of Your Own* failed to reach the Top Ten in America though the two year old track *Pinball Wizard* became a big hit in the U.K.

DJM were looking to their back catalogue to keep the demand satisfied but all they could find was a live LP recorded in 1974, titled *Here And There*. One side had been recorded at London's Royal Festival Hall and the other at New York's Madison Square Garden. It failed to capture the magic of Elton John in performance and remains simply a curio.

The first E.J. release on Rocket was a duet with Kiki Dee. *Don't Go Breaking My Heart* became his only British Number One single and its success

Leaving NY's Studio 54 (note the odd shoes and socks)

took him by surprise. A promo film shown on TV was the only glimpse British audiences would have of him that year as he devoted more and more time to his new responsibilities as chairman of Watford. Contemplating his inevitable withdrawal from the music business the previous year he had said 'I don't think there is anything rewarding in going on stage playing *Crocodile Rock* when I'm 35 or 40, and people going "oh, I remember him". I'm having a ball now. I get immense pleasure from what I'm doing...

'But I certainly ain't going to be appearing at Batley Variety Club or play the Talk of the Town when I'm 40, because there's more to life than that. You have to realise you can only reach a certain peak. One day it's going to just tail off slightly, moderately or heavily. I'm quite prepared for that to happen. You have to be prepared to do other things.' With his recording output now fully under his own control and his ambitions fulfilled beyond his dreams, that day had finally arrived.

Punk was bursting onto the British music scene and Elton saw no place in its angry new world for him. His autumn offering was another double LP. *Blue Moves* made its appearance in October '76 but the media, ever anxious for good copy, was too busy encouraging the Sex Pistols with limitless space to bother with the Soweto Riots, the Olympic Games and Mao Tse-Tung's death never mind the new album from Elton John.

Battling against indifference, the album and the single taken from it, *Sorry Seems To Be The Hardest Word* clambered up the U.K. charts but in America where his popularity remained high it peaked at Number Three. But the glory days were over. One year later he would split with Bernie Taupin as the distances between them made an on-going writing partnership impractical.

This period was later explained on the 1980 LP *21 at 33* in the song *Two Rooms At The End Of The World*. Two more singles were culled from *Blue Moves*, the minor hit *Crazy Water* in February '77 and the dance orientated *Bite Your Lip*. At nearly seven minutes in length the latter had a hard time getting airplay. Whereas before Elton's popularity had demanded his records automatic inclusion on the playlists this time he had to make way for the glut of new names clambering over each other for airtime. Unlike his friend Bolan and several other glam rockers looked on by the punks as godfathers of trash, Elton did not embrace the new movement.

Except for the odd promotional sortie for the most part of '77 and '78 Elton took up his Watford scarf and retired to the directors' box at Vicarage Road.

8 | A SINGLE

MAN

For the greater part of '77 and '78 Elton retired behind the electrified fences of his Windsor mansion. John Reid remembers 'At one point I honestly began to think he was in danger of turning into a recluse.' The only record release of '77 was *Greatest Hits Volume II*. It included his only U.K. Number One (the duet with Kiki Dee) as well as two cover versions *Lucy In The Sky With Diamonds* and *Pinball Wizard*. Another song on the LP was *Sorry Seems To Be The Hardest Word* which had already become a standard. Frank Sinatra sang it at the Royal Albert Hall and had Elton take a bow.

Another track from the LP, *Chameleon*, had been written for the Beach Boys. So pleased was Elton by his commission that instead of taking his usual half an hour he polished the song over a period of six months! But his dedication was in vain as the Californians rejected the track when they heard it. Undeterred Elton recorded it himself, and felt pleased with the result. It had summed up how he felt about the band.

One trip he treated himself to was a journey to the States but this time it wasn't to play. While there he engineered a meeting with the ultimate recluse Elvis Presley. 'I was introduced to him and there in front of me was this gross figure starring back at me, blankly. I knew immediately that he was going to die. "You're not long for this world" I thought to myself. He had destruction written all over him. When I heard that he had died it didn't surprise me at all. It was as if he was just waiting for it to happen. He had let everthing get out of control somehow and there was no way things could have turned out differently. I'm damned sure it's not going to happen to me.'

Even though he remained active through endless games of tennis with sporting friends Elton could not halt the problem of a receding hairline. The problem became so acute that in September '77 he flew to Paris for the first of six hair transplants. The one consolation for him was that his wealth allowed him the best treatment and the best 'surgeon' — Dr. Pierre Pouteaux.

The method Elton chose was unique to the French and was termed square grafting. It involved removing a tiny patch of hair bearing scalp, cutting it into smaller pieces and then grafting them back on to help spread growth. Said a leading expert 'It is less wasteful on hairs than the older system of taking circles of scalp. But it can't work miracles.'

Another five such 'operations' were believed to have been needed over the next six years and meanwhile Elton hid his embarrassment beneath a splendid array of hats. A spokesman for the surgeon explained 'The hats were Elton's way of hiding from a big problem for him. Prior to the operation he was nearly bald as an egg and terribly self conscious about it. To begin with he wore hats just to cover the scars, then it developed into part of his image and his trademark — even though the surgeon had told him to expose his head as much as possible.'

His absence from the music scene saw a decline in his popularity and this was accelerated by reports of his flirtation with disco. He recorded four tracks with Thom Bell in Seattle. Bell had

(above) Jimmy Hill, comedian Eric Morecombe and Elton at a charity gala in May '78

(bottom right) Elton is awarded a 'platinum ticket' by Madison Square Garden for having attracted an audience of over 250,000

worked with The Stylistics and The Detroit Spinners and seemed an unlikely choice of partner. The tapes were shelved until 1979 when three were remixed by Elton and released on a 12 inch. The fourth, *Shine On Through* remains unreleased though a re-recording of the same song appeared on the next album, *A Single Man*. Two of the songs from the Bell sessions had been written by Bell and James, a third by Elton and Bernie and the fourth by Elton and his new lyric partner Gary Osbourne. The Detroit Spinners sang backing vocals on *Are You Ready For Love*. Elton still believes the sessions were the right thing to do at the time if only because Bell encouraged him to sing in a lower register and so increase his vocal range. The mixes though were 'too sweet' for Elton's taste.

For most of '78 he found himself couped up in the recording studio co-producing Rocket acts,

90

(above) With Paul and Linda McCartney collecting Capital Radio Music Awards for 1977

(page 94/5) Elton meets Kiss

Blue and China, with Clive Franks. Franks had been Elton's sound mixer on every tour since 1972. As Elton worked more closely with Franks so he grew apart from Gus Dudgeon, who eventually left his directorship at Rocket and in the ensuing confusion the company almost foundered. The situation was not helped by an unhealthy drain on their financial resources caused by Blue and China's failure as hitmakers. In the midst of this crisis Elton switched roles and began work on his new album *A Single Man* with Franks as producer.

But the first result of this new partnership was a disastrous single *Ego*, a two year old song and the last Taupin/John A-side for three and a half years.

A Single Man was released in October '78. All the songs had been written by Elton and Gary Osbourne with the exception of *Song For Guy*, which Elton had penned himself. That track had been written and recorded in one day but remained un-titled until the next when Rocket's messenger boy, Guy Burchett was killed during a Sunday run on his motorbike. Elton knew the song was 'a death song' but had been at a loss for a title.

The cover for the LP was taken just down the road from Elton's Windsor home. He had felt lazy that day so he and the photographer drove the few miles to Windsor Castle, hustling picnickers out of view of the lens and created the cover in an afternoon.

When the next single *Part Time Love* was released the pressures and anxieties associated with Rocket piled up and he had a heart attack scare. He was admitted to hospital but was found to be suffering from nervous exhaustion. In the interim, sales of the single leapt up from 3,000 a day to 20,000 per day. He later quipped that having a heart attack scare was a great way to increase sales! On recovering he threw himself totally into the task of helping Watford rise from the fourth division.

In June '83 when touring China with the club he paid tribute to them for saving his sanity during this lull in his career. 'These people saved me,' he said. 'If the chance hadn't come I'd have gone home to my big house in Windsor, locked myself behind the big steel gates and I don't know what would have happened . . . sometimes I'd arrive at the club in ridiculous gaudy clothes — shoes built up so I was six foot three. Pink hair. They might have sniggered behind my back but they've tolerated me until I've had time to mature.'

Apart from a few isolated incidents when he first joined the board the reaction from other directors and other clubs has been polite and encouraging. Most seem to respect his dedication and genuine love for the game. He maintains a good rapport with all the players, taking trouble to memorise their wives names but keeping a distance socially so as not to upset manager Graham Taylor's discipline.

An immediate problem that brought him to earth and made him 'politically aware' was the need to build a new ground. No matter how famous he had become or how much weight he had in the music business, when it came to asking Watford Council for permission he was left in no doubt as to who held the power. Permission was refused and Elton suspected the Council had envisaged him paying for the stadium out of his own pocket. In the end the old ground was extended. Elton remains adamant that the chairmanship of Watford is every bit as important as his music and that it is a job for life.

Despite falling sales and commitments to his beloved team E.J. couldn't resist the call of the road. In January '79 he announced a return to live work beginning with a 'solo comeback tour' which he titled 'A Single Man Plus Ray Cooper'. There was to be no backing band, just Elton and Ray, the they

Not a morbid person he did have a penchant for solemn music citing the *Enigma Variations* as a favourite example.

Song For Guy became Elton's only instrumental hit to date when it was released in November '78. Originally there had been no plans to make an album. Elton had returned to the studio to record *Ego* and its B-side *Shine On Through* but as he hadn't written for so long the melodies spewed forth at a tremendous rate, and Franks was there to produce them. It hadn't been Elton's intention to leave Bernie Taupin out of it but Taupin was in the States and Osbourne was only on the other side of the control room window.

Pictured during a visit to the USA in October, 1980

would undertake a six week tour beginning in Europe and ending with a series of concerts in Russia. The idea being to play all of the countries he had not yet conquered. These included France, Belgium, Spain, Israel, Ireland and of course the USSR. Where Elton took the opportunity to play less familiar numbers such as *Come Down In Time* and *Ticking*. He was later to say that Ray had been the only person with whom he could have done such a tour because Ray was a tremendously exuberant character. Despite the limitations of

being a duo they still managed to put on a good show and on a personal level Elton claimed that Ray had taught him a lot during the tour and had been a great friend during bouts of depression. Ray was an ex-RADA student whose career as an actor continued while he was a member of Elton's band. Though by the time *21 at 33* was being recorded he had left to appear in Robert Altman's film version of *Popeye*.

The Moscow show was broadcast live by BBC Radio One to listeners in the UK and the complete tour was filmed for theatrical release and titled *From Russia With Elton*. What began as a low key tour of Europe for the purpose of getting him back into the idea of performing again, developed into an historic journey behind the Iron Curtain. The Russians even invited Elton's parents for the ten day tour. They were treated royally, though the audience at Moscow's Rossya hall were at first unresponsive to Western rock. Only later was it revealed that 95% of the audience were dignitaries. Against Elton's wishes only 5% of the tickets had been offered to the public. Feelings ran high throughout his time there. In one incident fans gathered along the route and tossed presents into his carriage as the train sped from Leningrad to Moscow. Elton, his mother, and even a hardened journalist who had accompanied them from London, were in tears at this display of feelings. All three could guess how much these people had paid for the gifts on the black market.

As much as he would like to return there Elton has clearly stated that he will not entertain the idea as long as the Russians occupy Afghanistan. On his return his twentieth LP was released. *Victim Of Love* had been recorded in Munich and was produced by Peter Bellotte with whom Elton had been friendly since Bluesology played the Top Ten Club in Hamburg. Bellotte had been involved with Donna Summer's career and had approached Elton after the latter's Drury Lane concert when he offered to produce a disco LP. Elton wanted 'to do a Lennon'. He had decided to put himself into the hands of the producer. He would let him supply the songs (all but one were co-written by Bellotte) he would leave the backing tracks to Bellotte (Elton didn't play a note on this LP), all he wanted to do was sing. It was a bad move. All the vocals had been done in eight hours *Victim Of Love* was not disco at its best.

Elton later admitted it was just the first in a string of such self-indulgences. The LP flopped and his sales hit an all time low. He was accused of jumping on the disco bandwagon, a criticism not altogether unwarranted. Rod Stewart had just released *Do Ya Think I'm Sexy* and The Rolling Stones had even got in on the act with *Miss You*. Despite the hammering it received Elton remained unrepentant. 'I'm not ashamed of it' he countered.

Not having been required to write for the album it meant that another LP could follow only six months later. The songs for his twenty-first LP *21 At 33* were written in Grasse and it was significant for three reasons. The first was that it reunited him with Bernie Taupin who supplied the lyrics for three of the tracks, the second was that on it he experimented by writing with other well-known songwriters, Judy Tzuke and Tom Robinson, and finally, through his collaboration with the latter,

he revealed he was gay. A fact not particularly significant in itself (except of course to Elton) but it did lead to a terrible drop in his popularity in America and that must have hurt him far more.

The subject had come up during an interview with the American magazine Rolling Stone. He later recalled 'When I first talked about it it affected my popularity in the States far more than in Britain. There are far more maniacally religious people here (USA). The British public on the other hand like you to be more upfront. They don't make such issues into big deals.' Friends and fans couldn't care less of course and rallied around to give him support. Rod Stewart remembers 'I think I saw him at his lowest ebb after he did an interview with Rolling Stone magazine in which he admitted being gay. I think that was probably a turning point in his career too, but he won't admit that. I still can't see why he admitted that. Perhaps he needed to get that statement off his shoulder and let everybody know.'

Support also came from the somewhat unlikely quarter of Watford football club. A couple of years later Elton confessed 'I was going through a stage about two years ago when I was drinking quite heavily and letting myself go physically. Graham (Taylor) took one look at me and said "Come round to my house tomorrow morning." I did and he immediately took out a bottle of brandy and put it on the table in front of me. He said "Go on, open it, that's what you really want, isn't it". In that second I saw what I was doing to myself and pulled myself together.'

Being chairman also meant he wasn't allowed the wasteful luxury of wallowing in self-pity. 'As chairman I was forced to do things I never had to do before because I'd always had someone to do them for me ... it brought home to me how helpless I had become. I'll never forget the first away game for which I made my own travel arrangements. I bought my own tickets, booked my own hotel, got there on time, checked in by myself. The sense of elation was terrific. I said to myself, "There you are, you see, you daft sod – you're thirty odd years old and you can do it if you want to"'

Three singles had been culled from the *21 At 33* album. The first, *Little Jeannie*, had reached Number Three in the U.S. charts prior to the publication of the Rolling Stone interview, after which the second and third singles, *Don't Ya Wanna Play This Game No More (Sartorial Eloquence)* and *Nobody Wins* both flopped. In the UK *Little Jeannie* became a minor hit and the two singles which followed it *Sartorial Eloquence* and *Dear God* failed to make any significant impact.

I'M STILL

On 16 January 1981 it was announced that Elton was to be top of the bill at Prince Andrew's birthday party. It was originally intended as a joint celebration for Prince Andrew's twenty-first and Prince Phillip's sixtieth to be held at Windsor Castle at the end of the month. As it turned out the party was delayed until June, which meant Elton would have to travel 7,000 miles from Los Angeles to be there.

Touring commitments meant he would have to return the next day! No wonder he left before the 4 am breakfast. He was however 'absolutely delighted' at the invitation. As for the fee: his agents said 'It depends on the circumstances. For an artist of his calibre, it could be anything from nothing to £100,000. I would imagine that Elton would do it for free.'

The event eventually took place on 20 June and the highlight was Elton's hour long set. One of the four hundred guests remarked 'He was absolutely thrilled about being there and I think Andy was delighted he could make it.' Despite the royal patronage he was having trouble with MCA in the States. In March he had filed a suit for five and a half million pounds because the company had allegedly refused to release his next album *The Fox*. The company countered by claiming that three of the tracks had already been singles and that another was a reworking of an old song.

Elton was plainly upset and claimed that the choice of tracks rested solely with him. The result of all this was that he switched labels to Geffen and *The Fox* was released in its intended form in May. The album was produced by Chris Thomas and recorded in London, LA and Nice. It gave him two minor hits, *Nobody Wins* and *Just Like Belgium*.

The former was a French song written by Jean Paul Dreau with lyrics by Gary Osbourne. Elton had first heard it on the radio while motoring through France and then he searched the record shops to no avail. It eventually came to light in a French street market 'next to the courgettes'! It became his first French Number One and the occasion happily coincided with his 34th birthday.

STANDING

Phonogram (with whom Rocket were now affiliated) gave a party in his honour and presented him with a new oil painting. The guests included Rod Stewart and Pete Townsend. The Who's innovative axeman was guesting on Elton's then current sessions.

The album had been slated by the critics somewhat unfairly and amidst the ballyhoo he again contemplated retirement. 'Everyone wants to knock me down these days. But I've now decided that I'll always bounce back . . . now I've got my self respect back I've given up worrying about critics. I only do things for my fans these days.'

Another track from the album, *Elton's Song* caused few ripples when heard in the context of the LP, but when a film was made of it the following year for inclusion on a video album it caused a furore. The song had been written with Tom Robinson, an artist noted for his stand on gay rights and who undoubtedly helped Elton come to terms with his own homosexuality. It concerned a schoolboy's crush on an older boy and though hardly the first song on the subject and certainly not the last, it still managed to outrage the headmaster in whose exclusive public school it had been filmed.

The headmaster of Stowe School in Buckinghamshire, Christopher Turner, claimed he had not been shown the lyrics of the song and that a synopsis of the shooting script had been deliberately watered down to mislead him. After a national newspaper gave him and the school chaplain a private screening of the film they claimed that 'It will cause great offence to the old boys and parents of the children here. We will have to call a meeting of the governors and then consider what legal action we can take.'

The leader of the pack of scouts who took part in the film said 'I thought it was going to be a straight forward Elton John video. I was conned like everyone else.' Film-makers Russell Mulcahy, and Keith Williams admitted to watering down the script before showing it to the headmaster and the

end result was that the clip was cut from the English version of the tape.

Elton who had absolutely nothing whatsoever to do with the film said 'The song is on the American video but not the British one. I am very angry. It is a lovely innocent number and there is no reason to ban it.' And indeed there wasn't. The two professional actors who play the two boys do little but gaze into each others eyes. So much for his earlier belief in the liberal views of the 'British public . . . they don't make such issues into big deals.'

He must have wondered why he had bothered to admit his sexual preferences. Two unthinking New Zealand journalists teased him about it and were promptly punched by John Reid who was given a three week jail sentence for his trouble. Reid's loyalty is well noted. Glasgow born, he stood no nonsense from his employees and demanded loyalty and hard work.

He had once threatened Rocket executives with the sack if they didn't have short haircuts and wear smart business suits. When *Ego* failed to make the charts he fired two of them. Reid had started as a record plugger and became label manager for Motown by the time he was twenty-one. That's where he had first met Elton who recalls 'He was a dumpy balding little guy in a funny jump suit who used to go around cadging records.'

Though Dick James claims to have hired him, Reid says 'Dick James didn't know who I was until I walked into his office and asked for £10,000 a year to manage Elton John.' Despite his business acumen Reid admitted his years with Elton had been challenging and had taught him a lot. 'It took me a year to negotiate a contract for Elton with MCA Records in America. I had to take each stage slowly, I was dealing with people who had considerably more experience than I had.'

It had also been an extremely rewarding period. He has homes in Beverly Hills, Hollywood and a £300,000 mansion in Hertfordshire which boasts Princess Margaret as a 'regular visitor'. His companies are said to be worth £40 million and his gifts to Elton are on a generous scale. He once gave Elton a £20,000 watch.

Their partnership wasn't without its trouble though. 'We've ended up knocking each other around' claimed Reid. 'I've given him more than one black eye.' He added 'Oh yes, he's got a

(right) In Tunisia at the launch of Cartier's new spectacle range – other guests included Jane Birkin and Jacky Ickx

temper on him. You can see it coming. He'll smoulder and smoulder and then a little thing will spark it off and he'll hit the roof.'

In July '81 Reid sacked the entire staff at Rocket's London office. He had phoned just before two o'clock in the afternoon and when he found that all twenty-five were still at lunch he fired them there and then. One of the employees remarked 'When he couldn't talk to any of the people that he wanted to he had a fit. We are waiting to be removed from the building.' Only a few months earlier he had closed the LA office for 'financial reasons'.

Elton meanwhile, determined to show he may have been down but not out, had reformed the original three piece band with Dee and Nigel and underwent a gruelling worldwide tour. On his return from Australia he found himself with a hit single, *Blue Eyes* and a successful album *Jump Up*. 'This must be my lucky year. It's my first hit for six years.'

The distances involved hadn't prevented him from keeping up to date with Watford's progress. 'While I was away I phoned the club every day for up-to-the minute reports. I also listened to four matches live — all of which we won. It cost me a grand but it was worth every penny. I couldn't bear to be out of touch.'

One of the first things he did on his return was to buy two hundred and five original Goon Show scripts for £14,000 at Christie's. In doing so he saved these national treasures from going to the States. Asked why he had bought them he replied in his best Bluebottle accent 'I have but tem because I love tem.'

On a more serious note, the single *Empty Garden*, a tribute to John Lennon gunned down in December 1980, was released just prior to the album. Elton made his feelings known on the matter. 'Any loony can legally get his hands on a gun over there. I hate that.' He had earlier dismissed threats on his own life as the ramblings of 'cranks' and said defiantly 'no one will have a go at me. If they do, good luck to them. I am certainly not going around with a guard watching me all the time.'

When he performed *Empty Garden* in New York he was joined by Yoko Ono and her son Sean. Sean made a little speech thanking the crowd for their kind wishes and this little scene obviously left its mark on Elton's memory. Two months later he remarked 'I hope it will be possible for me to have children of my own at some time. If not by marriage then through adoption. I have always

Elton in America

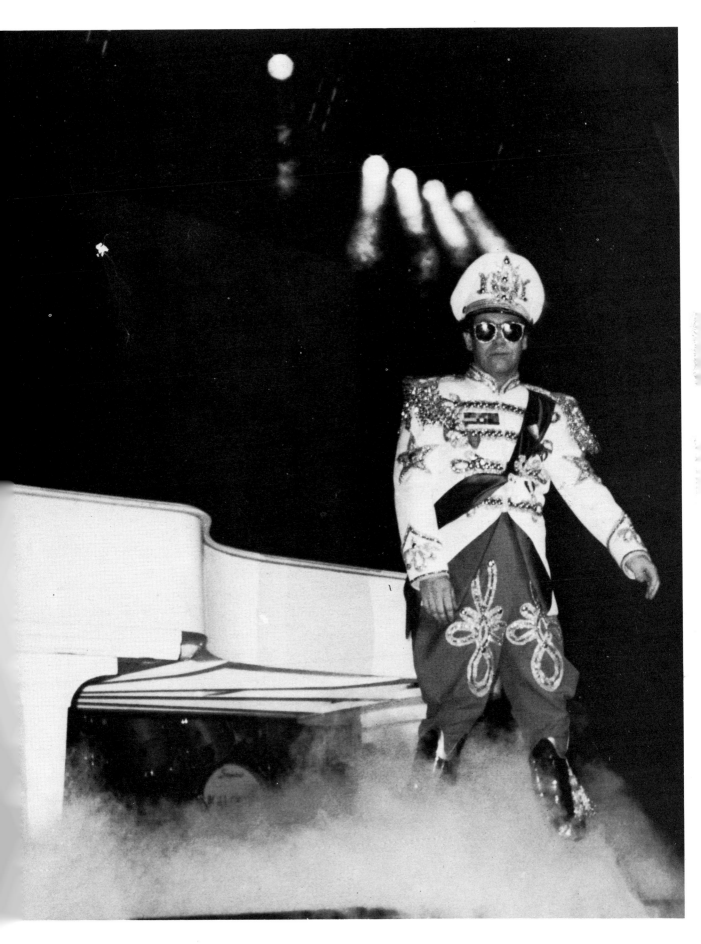

loved children and if I could have a son or daughter of my own it would give me so much happiness . . . my child would be the most important thing in my life.'

Jump Up also included a track called *Princess* which he dedicated to the Princess of Wales after meeting her at Prince Andrew's twenty-first birthday party. The songs had been written by Elton John and Bernie Taupin with the exception of four by John and Osbourne and one he wrote with Tim Rice. The album had been recorded in Monserratt, produced by Chris Thomas and featured on *Ball and Chain* was guitar hero Pete Townsend.

In the autumn he threw himself into an intense schedule of rehearsals in preparation for a UK tour, his first in three years, that would culminate in a record breaking fourteen nights at London's Hammersmith Odeon at Christmas. Although he had vowed in 1976 never to tour again he found it an easy decision to reconsider.

'I'm enjoying touring now more than ever and I figure that if I'm thirty five years old and still enjoying it, why not?' The tour opened in Newcastle on 4 November. 'I was nervous at first. Six years is a long time but it was fabulous. I couldn't have hoped for a better start.'

For the Christmas shows at Hammersmith Odeon he wrapped the entire building in lilac and green wrapping paper and a huge scarlet bow. The cost of this extravagance was £8,000 and a further £4,000 was spent on baubles and decorations for the inside. It was all a very welcome distraction from stifling business matters arising from an impending legal wrangle with DJM.

Before the writs began to fly in all directions Elton had praised Dick James for allowing Bernie and himself complete artistic freedom, including the choice of their record covers. When he hadn't understood their motives James still gave them room to experiment, and supported them at every turn.

In October it had been announced that Elton was sueing DJM for £30 million 'for the return of my musical copyright, rights to my recordings and damages.' It followed similar cases brought by Paul McCartney, Gilbert O'Sullivan and Sting. Said Stephen James 'he has caught the same disease.' And he added: 'We can't spend a lot of time and money in devloping recording artists to become successful, and having treated them fairly see them turn round after a period of years and attack you . . . no recording company will ever want to invest money in an artist again.' As for the songs he continued 'They would be of use to Elton John for emotional value and for more money from sales of his records and cover versions by other artists.'

(page 104) Leaving Mr Chow's restaurant in Knightsbridge after birthday celebrations
(above) On French tv June '83

The songs concerned number one hundred and fifty plus twenty five that had not been released. They dated from 1967 — 1975 and the future profits from sixteen albums also hung in the balance. James ended by saying 'If the court upholds this claim the music business is finished.'

There was no comment from Elton. After the London Christmas shows he took himself off to Monserratt once more to begin work on the new LP *Too Low For Zero*. He was naturally depressed over the legal wranglings and also unhappy about the performance of his current single *All Quiet On The Western Front*.

During the last Christmas show he preceded the song by claiming it was the slowest selling single in the history of MCA. He continued in the same vein on the island. 'In rock and roll it's all false. People are always swarming around you. It got so I could spot a phony after a minute.'

The new year began with Elton and Labour leader Michael Foot watching Elton's team beat Foot's favoured Plymouth Argyle 2 — 0. Watford had reached the hallowed first division the previous May after a game in Oslo. Elton remembered 'When Ross scored again I knew we were up and I felt really exhilarated. It really is a dream come true.' He had been quoted as saying 'I honestly believe that the first division is there for the asking . . . we are no longer a Cinderella club.' And there he was chairman of a first division club. No hopers in '76 rising to the first in a twist of fate that mirrored his own career in the late Seventies.

In March he announced that he would be taking four weeks off in the summer to tour China with the club. 'Partly to play football and partly to see the country.' That month he attended a party in Hollywood to honour the Queen and hit the headlines when he called it a 'disaster'. He complained 'It was so boring I fell asleep . . . it was a great shame the Queen didn't meet the real Hollywood and that the big Hollywood stars did not have a chance to meet her.' And he blamed singers Perry Como and Frank Sinatra for being 'under rehearsed.'

He was in Hollywood to audition for a part in a new comedy film. 'I've made a screen test with Liza Minnelli for a comedy film but I'll have to wait for the movie men to contact me before I know if it was any good. This is something I've wanted to do for a long time. I've been waiting for the right script. If everything goes according to plan I'll be filming in the autumn and that will take up all of my time. I have a new LP waiting for release so it's not as though I will be completely out of music.'

The film was to be directed by Blake Edwards who made *Arthur* with Minnelli and Dudley Moore and of course the *Pink Panther* films with the late Peter Sellers. 'I want to try to get into films' said Elton 'and I'm prepared to give up touring to have a go.'

He returned to England only to find that his house had been burgled and £56,000 worth of jewellery was missing. Police believed it had been an inside job as the thief had successfully negotiated electronically operated gates, guard dogs and alarms. The ironically title single *Guess That's Why They Call It The Blues* was then released and returned him to the charts courtesy of a great little video evoking the Fifties. Stevie Wonder was featured on harmonica.

The new album *Too Low For Zero* saw him reunited with Bernie. The two had last collaborated fully on *Blue Moves* seven years previously. Elton said the LP was 'very important for me, I've lived with it for so long and wouldn't change anything on it.' It took just three weeks to record and included ballads and rockers. The album spawned two more singles, *I'm Still Standing* and *Kiss The Bride*. All three were massive hits in England and the States and heralded a significant renaissance in his career: sales of the album now bring his total sales to date to over eighty million records worldwide.

In April he denied all knowledge of a planned concert in Paris. 'I don't know if it is a con or what it is, but I've got no concerts this year and I'm definitely not playing Paris on June 27. I'm devoting all my time to acting in a new film called *Hang Ups* with Liza Minnelli. It won't leave any time for concerts.'

The organisers explained 'This is no more than a simple misunderstanding.' Whatever the reasons, Elton's statement meant a restriction on all apprearances that year, with the exception of the planned trip to China. Watford were to play three matches against the national side.

The plane touched down in China on 30 May in the midst of a terrific heatwave. Elton stepped onto the tarmac in a three piece suit topped with a boater and though sweltering in the terminal building, kept his British cool.

Between matches there was time for a guided tour which included the Great Wall of China where he announced 'This is one of the few places I can go in the world without being recognised. I haven't known it for thirteen years.

'Chinese people look content to me. I'm settled in pretty handy with chopsticks and feel very much at home. I'm with my club and that's just as important to me as my career.' While there he laid a wreath at Mao Tse Tung's memorial and just prior to leaving spent £50,000 on antiques. 'It's the most enjoyable trip I've been on for a long time.'

The trip to China was Elton's way of restoring football's tarnished image abroad. Determined to stamp out the game's chief problem, hooliganism, he had even built a private railway station inside Watford's ground so that fans would be diverted from the town centre. On opening the £160,000 station he declared 'This is one way to combat hooliganism. It's the end of a headache.'

When the club transferred two of its players after the China trip, they offered to repay the £1,200,000 Elton had 'loaned' them over the past six years. He turned down the offer saying 'We have as many mountains to climb as when I first took over.' He suggested they use the transfer fee for a new stadium.

In August he flew to South Africa to play a series of dates including one with his old friend Rod Stewart at Sun City. He shrugged off the threat of blacklisting and vowed to return there. 'I'm not bothered . . . Sun City was magnificent and I'm going back.'

His gig with Rod was a warm up for their joint tour of the UK planned for Summer 1984. Said Elton 'We've been planning it for some time. It won't just be the two of us, on stage doing an hour each . . . We've been working together to produce a special show which will go on tour next summer.' And he added 'It will be slick, spectacular. It will hit everybody right between the eyes.'

'Eat your heart out, Jerry Lee'

Rod though had different plans. 'We could play for twenty minutes each, a sort of battle of the bands.' He entertained the idea of having two separate stages, one at each end of the hall so at the conclusion of one set the audience could turn round and watch the other.

The idea of a joint tour had begun as something of a joke. Rod recalls: 'It was one of those nights that we all dread. Freddy Mercury was there and the three of us had this idea of setting up a group called Teeth, Nose and Hair — it's not hard to guess which was which, is it — and going on the road together. Then later Elton and I talked and we decided the two of us should really do it.'

Like old vaudeville stars they took this opportunity to spar in public. 'They'll have to give us dressing rooms a hundred yards apart' joked Elton. 'He takes ages to get ready, he's so bloody finicky. He once checked out of the Dorchester because he said the sheets were too crisp. They grazed his elbows. So I sent him a silk nightdress with long sleeves. Soon afterwards I was supposed to meet him for dinner but didn't turn up because I was unwell. He sent me a wreath.'

Rod — 'I can't remember meeting the little squirt but he says he came up to me at a place called the Railway Hotel near Watford and asked for my autograph. He must have looked different then. He had some hair in those days.

'But we didn't really start to become close until he told me he was going to have to leave England for tax purposes back in 1975. I remember one night we were all round at my place in Windsor and I said to him "You bastard. How can you leave this great country?" I played him a video of the last night of The Proms. I showed him the FA Cup Final and I said "look at all this, how can you leave this?" Then two months later I was all packed up and gone!'

The John/Stewart tour will no doubt dominate the press adding more backstage stories to the lore of the road.

Although there are few records left for Elton to break or countries to conquer he will continue to tour and record into the Nineties if the public is still willing to listen. Elton is a universal talent whose music appeals to all age groups, colours and creeds.

As long as people need music to colour their lives, to make them dance, relax or comfort them in times of trouble the music of Elton John will remain alive. As he has said and proved in the past, when the time comes to retire for good he will happily do so, content in the knowledge that he has enriched the lives of millions and no artist could ask for more than that.

DISCOGRAPHY

UK SINGLES

COME BACK BABY/TIMES GETTING TOUGHER THAN TOUGH

(*Fontana TF 594*)
Released July 1965
Produced by Jack Baverstock
Engineered by David Voyde
Recorded at Philips Studios, London

MR FRANTIC/EVERYDAY (I HAVE THE BLUES)

(*Fontana TF 668*)
Released February 1966
Produced by Jack Baverstock
Engineered by David Voyde
Recorded at Philips Studios, London

SINCE I FOUND YOU BABY/JUST A LITTLE BIT

(*Polydor 56195*)
Released 5 October 1967
Produced by Kenny Lynch
Recorded at IBC Studios, London

I'VE BEEN LOVING YOU/HERE'S TO THE NEXT TIME

(*Philips BFI643*)
Released 1 March 1968
Produced by Caleb Quaye
Recorded at Dick James Studios, London

LADY SAMANTHA/ALL ACROSS THE HAVENS

(*Philips BF 1739*)
Released 17 January 1969
Produced by Steve Brown
Recorded at Dick James Studios, London

IT'S ME THAT YOU NEED/JUST LIKE STRANGE RAIN

(*DJM DJS 205*)
Released 16 May 1969
Produced by Steve Brown
Recorded at Olympic Studios, London

BORDER SONG/BAD SIDE OF THE MOON

(*DJM DJS 217*)
Released 20 March 1970
Produced by Gus Dudgeon
Recorded at Trident Studios, London

ROCK AND ROLL MADONNA/GREY SEAL

(*DJM DJS 22*)
Released 19 June 1970
Produced by Gus Dudgeon
Recorded at Trident Studios, London

YOUR SONG/INTO THE OLD MAN'S SHOES

(*DJM DJS 233*)
Released 7 January 1971
Produced by Gus Dudgeon
Recorded at Trident Studios, London

FRIENDS/HONEY ROLL

(*DJM DJS 244*)
Released 23 April 1971
Produced by Gus Dudgeon
Recorded at Trident Studios, London

ROCKET MAN/HOLIDAY INN/GOODBYE

(*DJM DJX 501*)
Released April 1972
Produced by Gus Dudgeon
Recorded at Strawberry Studios,
Chateau D'Hierouville

HONKY CAT/LADY SAMANTHA/IT'S ME THAT YOU NEED

(*DJM DJS 269*)
Released August 1972
Produced by Gus Dudgeon and Steve Brown
Recorded at Strawberry Studios, Chateau D'Hierouville
& Dick James Studios, London

CROCODILE ROCK/ELDERBERRY WINE

(*DJM DJS 271*)
Released 27 October 1972
Produced by Gus Dudgeon
Recorded at Strawberry Studios, Chateau
D'Hierouville, France

DANIEL/SKYLINE PIGEON

(*DJM DJS 275*)
Released January 1973
Produced by Gus Dudgeon
Recorded at Strawberry Studios, Chateau
D'Hierouville, France

SATURDAY NIGHT'S ALRIGHT FOR FIGHTING/JACK RABBIT/WHENEVER YOU'RE READY (WE'LL GO STEADY AGAIN)

(*DJM SJX 502*)
Released 29 June 1973
Produced by Gus Dudgeon
Recorded at Strawberry Studios, Chateau
D'Hierouville, France

GOODBYE YELLOW BRICK ROAD/SCREW YOU

(*DJM SJS 285*)
Released 7 September 1973
Produced by Gus Dudgeon
Recorded at Strawberry Studios, Chateau
D'Hierouville, France

STEP INTO CHRISTMAS/HO! HO! HO! WHO'D BE A TURKEY AT CHRISTMAS

(*DJM SJS 290*)
Released 26 November 1973
Produced by Gus Dudgeon
Recorded at Trident Studios, London

CANDLE IN THE WIND/BENNIE AND THE JETS

(*DJM DJS 297*)
Released February 1974
Produced by Gus Dudgeon
Recorded at Strawberry Studios, Chateau
D'Hierouville, France

DON'T LET THE SUN GO DOWN ON ME/SICK CITY

(*DJM DJS 302*)
Released May 1974
Produced by Gus Dudgeon
Recorded at Caribou Ranch, Colorado, USA

THE BITCH IS BACK/COLD HIGHWAY

(*DJM DJS 322*)
Released 30 August 1974
Produced by Gus Dudgeon
Recorded at Caribou Ranch, Colorado, USA

LUCY IN THE SKY WITH DIAMONDS/ONE DAY AT A TIME

(*DJM DJS 340*)
Released 15 November 1974
Produced by Gus Dudgeon
Recorded at Caribou Ranch, Colorado, USA

PHILADELPHIA FREEDOM/I SAW HER STANDING THERE

(*DJM DJS 354*)
Released 28 February 1975
Produced by Gus Dudgeon
Recorded at Caribou Ranch, Colorado, USA

ISLAND GIRL/SUGAR ON THE FLOOR

(*DJM DJS 610*)
Released 19 September 1975
Produced by Gus Dudgeon
Recorded at Caribou Ranch, Colorado, USA

GROW SOME FUNK OF YOUR OWN/I FEEL LIKE A BULLET IN THE GUN OF ROBERT FORD

(*DJM DJS 629*)
Released 9 January 1976
Produced by Gus Dudgeon
Recorded at Caribou Ranch, Colorado, USA

PINBALL WIZARD/HARMONY

(*DJM DJS 652*)
Released 12 March 1976
Produced by Gus Dudgeon
Recorded at Ramport Studios, London and Strawberry Studios, Chateau D'Hierouville, France

DON'T GO BREAKING MY HEART/SNOW QUEEN

(*Rocket ROKN 512*)
Released 12 June 1976
Produced by Gus Dudgeon
Recorded at Eastern Sound, Toronto

BENNY AND THE JETS/ROCK AND ROLL MADONNA

(*DJM DJS 10705*)
Released 9 September 1976
Produced by Gus Dudgeon
Recorded at Strawberry Studios, Chateau D'Hierouville, France and Trident Studios, London

SORRY SEEMS TO BE THE HARDEST WORD/SHOULDER HOLSTER

(*Rocket ROKN 517*)
Released 10 October 1976
Produced by Gus Dudgeon
Recorded at Eastern Sound, Toronto

CRAZY WATER/CHAMELEON

(*Rocket ROKN 521*)
Released 4 February 1977
Produced by Gus Dudgeon
Recorded at Eastern Sound, Toronto

THE GOALDIGGER SONG/JIMMY, BRIAN, ELTON, ERIC

(*Rocket GOALD 1*)
Released April 1977
Produced by Elton John

YOUR SONG/ROCKET MAN/SATURDAY NIGHT'S ALRIGHT FOR FIGHTING/WHENEVER YOU'RE READY WE'LL GO STEADY AGAIN

(*DJM DJR 18001*)
Released 17 May 1977
Produced by Gus Dudgeon
Recorded at Trident Studios, London and Strawberry Studios, Chateau D'Hierouville, France

BITE YOUR LIP (GET UP AND DANCE)/CHICAGO

(*Rocket ROKN 526*)
Released 3 June 1977
Produced by Gus Dudgeon
Recorded at Eastern Sound, Toronto

EGO/FLINTSTONE BOY

(*Rocket ROKN 538*)
Released 21 March 1978
Produced by Elton John/Clive Franks
Recorded at The Mill at Cookham, Berks.

FUNERAL FOR A FRIEND/LOVE LIES BLEEDING/WE ALL FALL IN LOVE SOMETIMES/CURTAINS

(*DJM DJT 15000*)
Released 16 September 1978
Produced by Gus Dudgeon
Recorded at Strawberry Studios, Chateau D'Hierouville, France and Caribou Ranch, Colorado, USA

LADY SAMANTHA/SKYLINE PIGEON

(*DJM DJS 10901*)
Released 18 September 1978
Produced by Steve Brown
Recorded at Dick James Studios, London

YOUR SONG/BORDER SONG

(*DJM DJS 10902*)
Released 18 September 1978
Produced by Gus Dudgeon
Recorded at Trident Studios, London

HONKY CAT/SIXTY YEARS ON

(*DJM DJS 10903*)
Released 18 September 1978
Produced by Gus Dudgeon
Recorded at Strawberry Studios, Chateau D'Hierouville, France and Trident Studios, London

COUNTRY COMFORT/CROCODILE ROCK

(*DJM DJS 10904*)
Released 18 September 1978
Produced by Gus Dudgeon
Recorded at Trident Studios, London and Strawberry Studios, Chateau D'Hierouville, France

ROCKET MAN (I THINK IT'S GONNA BE A LONG LONG TIME)/DANIEL

(*DJM DJS 10905*)
Released 18 September 1978
Produced by Gus Dudgeon
Recorded at Strawberry Studios, Chateau D'Hierouville, France

SWEET PAINTED LADY/GOODBYE YELLOW BRICK ROAD

(*DJM DJS 10906*)
Released 18 September 1978
Produced by Gus Dudgeon
Recorded at Strawberry Studios, Chateau D'Hierouville, France

PHILADELPHIA FREEDOM/LUCY IN THE SKY WITH DIAMONDS

(*DJM DJS 10911*)
Released 18 September 1978
Produced by Gus Dudgeon
Recorded at Caribou Ranch, Colorado, USA

CANDLE IN THE WIND/I FEEL LIKE A BULLET (IN THE GUN OF ROBERT FORD)

(*DJM DJS 10908*)
Released 18 September 1978
Produced by Gus Dudgeon
Recorded at Strawberry Studios, Chateau D'Hierouville, France and Caribou Ranch, Colorado, USA

DON'T LET THE SUN GO DOWN ON ME/SOMEONE SAVED MY LIFE TONIGHT

(*DJM DJS 10907*)
Released 18 September 1978
Produced by Gus Dudgeon
Recorded at Caribou Ranch, Colorado, USA

THE BITCH IS BACK/GROW SOME FUNK OF YOUR OWN

(*DJM DJS 10909*)
Released 18 September 1978
Produced by Gus Dudgeon
Recorded at Caribou Ranch, Colorado, USA

ISLAND GIRL/SATURDAY NIGHT'S ALRIGHT FOR FIGHTING

(*DJM DJS 10910*)
Released 18 September 1978
Produced by Gus Dudgeon
Recorded at Caribou Ranch, Colorado, USA

PINBALL WIZARD/BENNY AND THE JETS

(*DJM DJS 10912*)
Released 18 September 1978
Produced by Gus Dudgeon
Recorded at Ramport Studio, London

PART-TIME LOVE/I CRY AT NIGHT

(*Rocket XPRESS 1*)
Released 4 October 1978
Produced by Elton John/Clive Franks
Recorded at The Mill, Cookham, Berks.

SONG FOR GUY/LOVESICK

(*Rocket XPRESS 5*)
Released 28 November 1978
Produced by Elton John/Clive Franks
Recorded at The Mill, Cookham, Berks.

ARE YOU READY FOR LOVE/ARE YOU READY FOR LOVE

(*Rocket XPRESS 13*)
Released 30 April 1979
Produced by Thom Bell
Recorded at Sigma & Sound Studios, Philadelphia and Kay Smith Studio, Seattle.

ARE YOU READY FOR LOVE/THREE WAY LOVE AFFAIR/MAMA CAN'T BUY YOU LOVE

(*Rocket XPRESS 13-12*)
Released 30 April 1979
Produced by Thom Bell
Recorded at Sigma & Sound Studios, Philadelphia and Kay Smith Studio, Seattle

MAMA CAN'T BUY YOU LOVE/STRANGERS

(*Rocket XPRESS 20*)
Released August 1979
Produced by Thom Bell
Recorded at Kay Smith Studio, Seattle

VICTIM OF LOVE/STRANGERS

(*Rocket XPRESS 21*)
Released 14 September 1979
Produced by Pete Bellotte, Elton John/Clive Franks
Recorded at Musicland, Munich

JOHNNY B. GOODE/THUNDER IN THE NIGHT

(*Rocket XPRESS 24-12*)
Released December 1979
Produced by Pete Bellote
Recorded at Musicland, Munich

JOHNNY B. GOODE/THUNDER IN THE NIGHT

(*Rocket XPRESS 24*)
Released December 1979
Produced by Pete Bellotte
Recorded at Musicland, Munich

LITTLE JEANNIE/CONQUER THE SUN

(*Rocket XPRESS 32*)
Released 1 May 1980
Produced by Elton John/Clive Franks
Recorded at Superbear Studios, Nice

SARTORIAL ELOQUENCE/WHITE MAN DANGER/CARTIER

(*Rocket XPRESS 41*)
Released 5 August 1980
Produced by Elton John/Clive Franks
Recorded at Superbear Studios, Nice

HARMONY/MONA LISAS AND MAD HATTERS

(*DJM DJS 10961*)
Released 1 November 1980
Produced by Gus Dudgeon
Recorded at Strawberry Studios, Chateau
D'Hierouville, France

DEAR GOD/TACTICS/STEAL AWAY CHILD/LOVE SO COLD

(*Rocket ELTON 1*)
Released 14 November 1980
Produced by Elton John/Clive Franks
Recorded at Superbear Studios, Nice

I SAW HER STANDING THERE/WHATEVER GETS YOU THROUGH THE NIGHT/LUCY IN THE SKY WITH DIAMONDS

(*DJM DJS 10965*)
Released 13 March 1981
Produced by Gus Dudgeon
Recorded at Madison Square Garden

NOBODY WINS/FOOLS IN FASHIONS

(*Rocket XPRESS 54*)
Released 8 May 1981
Produced by Chris Thomas, Elton John/Clive Franks
Recorded at Sunset Sound, Los Angeles

JUST LIKE BELGIUM/CAN'T GET OVER GETTING OVER LOSING YOU

(*Rocket XPRESS 59*)
Released 3 July 1981
Produced by Chris Thomas, Elton John/Clive Franks
Recorded at Superbear Studios, Nice and Sunset
Sound, Los Angeles.

LOVING YOU IS SWEETER THAN EVER (with Kiki Dee)/(B-side by Kiki Dee)

(*Ariola ARO 269*)
Released November 1981
Produced by Pip Williams

BLUE EYES/HEY PAPA LEGBA

(*Rocket XPRESS 71*)
Released March 1982
Produced by Chris Thomas
Recorded at AIR Studios, Monserrat

EMPTY GARDEN/TAKE ME DOWN TO THE OCEAN

(*Rocket XPRESS 77*)
Released May 1982
Produced by Chris Thomas (B-side by Elton John and
Clive Franks)
Recorded at AIR Studios, Monserrat
Also released as a picture disc (XPPIC 77)

PRINCESS/THE RETREAT

(*Rocket XPRESS 85*)
Released September 1982
Produced by Chris Thomas
Recorded at AIR Studios, Monserrat

I GUESS THAT'S WHY THEY CALL IT THE BLUES/CHOC-ICE GOES MENTAL

(*Rocket XPRESS 91*)
Released April 1983
Produced by Chris Thomas
Recorded at AIR Studios, Monserrat

I'M STILL STANDING/EARN WHILE YOU LEARN

(*Rocket EJS 1*)
Released July 1983
Produced by Chris Thomas
Recorded at AIR Studios, Monserrat
Also released as a 12″ (EJS 112) and a picture disc
(EJPIC 1)

KISS THE BRIDE/DREAMBOAT

(*Rocket EJS 2*)
Released October 1983
Produced by Chris Thomas
Recorded at AIR Studios, Monserrat
Also released as a 12″ (EJS 212), and in double pack
along with EGO/Song For Guy (EJS 222)

COLD AS CHRISTMAS (IN THE MIDDLE OF THE YEAR)/CRYSTAL

(*Rocket EJS 3*)
Released December 1983
Produced by Chris Thomas
Recorded at AIR Studios, Monserrat
Also released as a 12″ with the extra track JE VEUX DE LA
TENDRESSE (EJS 312), and in a double pack along with
DON'T GO BREAKING MY HEART/SNOW QUEEN
(both with Kiki Dee) (EJS 33)

SAD SONGS (SAY SO MUCH)/A SIMPLE MAN

(*Rocket PH 7*)
Released May 1984
Produced by Chris Thomas
Recorded at AIR Studios, Monserrat
Also released as a 12″ (PH 12)

PASSENGERS (REMIX)/LONELY BOY

(*Rocket EJS 5*)
Released August 1984
Produced by Chris Thomas
Recorded at AIR Studios, Monserrat
Also released as a 12″ (EJS 512) with the extra track
BLUE EYES

US SINGLES

LADY SAMANTHA/ALL ACROSS THE HAVENS

(*DJM 70008*)
Released January 1969
Produced by Steve Brown
Recorded at Dick James Studios, London

LADY SAMANTHA/IT'S ME THAT YOU NEED

(*Congress C6017*)
Released January 1970
Produced by Steve Brown
Recorded at Dick James Studios, London

BORDER SONG/BAD SIDE OF THE MOON

(*Congress C6022*)
Released April 1970
Produced by Gus Dudgeon
Recorded at Trident Studios, London

FROM DENVER TO L.A./WARM SUMMER RAIN

(*Viking 1010*)
Released 1970
Produced by Christian Gaubert
Recorded at Olympic Studios, London

BORDER SONG/BAD SIDE OF THE MOON

(*UNI 55246*)
Released September 1970
Produced by Gus Dudgeon
Recorded at Trident Studios, London

TAKE ME TO THE PILOT/YOUR SONG

(*UNI 55264*)
Released 26 October 1970
Produced by Gus Dudgeon
Recorded at Trident Studios, London

FRIENDS/ HONEY ROLL

(*UNI 55277*)
Released 5 March 1971
Produced by Gus Dudgeon
Recorded at Trident Studios, London

LEVON/ GOODBYE

(*UNI 55314*)
Released 29 November 1971
Produced by Gus Dudgeon
Recorded at Trident Studios, London

TINY DANCER/ RAZOR FACE

(*UNI 55318*)
Released 7 February 1972
Produced by Gus Dudgeon
Recorded at Trident Studios, London

ROCKET MAN/ SUZIE (DRAMAS)

(*UNI 55328*)
Released 17 April 1972
Produced by Gus Dudgeon
Recorded at Strawberry Studios, Chateau
D'Hierouville, France

HONKY CAT/ SLAVE

(*UNI 55343*)
Released 31 July 1972
Produced by Gus Dudgeon
Recorded at Strawberry Studios, Chateau
D'Hierouville, France

CROCODILE ROCK/ELDERBERRY WINE

(*MCA 40000*)
Released 20 November 1972
Produced by Gus Dudgeon
Recorded at Strawberry Studios, Chateau
D'Hierouville, France

DANIEL/SKYLINE PIGEON

(*MCA 40046*)
Released 26 March 1973
Produced by Gus Dudgeon
Recorded at Strawberry Studios, Chateau
D'Hierouville, France

SATURDAY NIGHT'S ALRIGHT FOR FIGHTING/JACK RABBIT/WHENEVER YOU'RE READY (WE'LL GO STEADY AGAIN)

(*MCA 40105*)
Released 16 July 1973
Produced by Gus Dudgeon
Recorded at Strawberry Studios, Chateau
D'Hierouville, France

GOODBYE YELLOW BRICK ROAD/YOUNG MAN'S BLUES

(*MCA 40148*)
Released 15 October 1973
Produced by Gus Dudgeon
Recorded at Strawberry Studios, Chateau
D'Hierouville, France

STEP INTO XMAS/HO! HO! HO! WHO'D BE A TURKEY AT CHRISTMAS

(*MCA 65018*)
Released 26 November 1973
Produced by Gus Dudgeon
Recorded at Trident Studios, London

BENNIE AND THE JETS/HARMONY

(*MCA 40198*)
Released 4 February 1974
Produced by Gus Dudgeon
Recorded at Strawberry Studios, Chateau
D'Hierouville, France

DON'T LET THE SUN GO DOWN ON ME/SICK CITY

(*MCA 40259*)
Released May 1974
Produced by Gus Dudgeon
Recorded at Caribou Ranch, Colorado, USA

THE BITCH IS BACK/COLD HIGHWAY

(*MCA 40297*)
Released 3 September 1974
Produced by Gus Dudgeon
Recorded at Caribou Ranch, Colorado, USA

LUCY IN THE SKY WITH DIAMONDS/ONE DAY AT A TIME

(*MCA 40344*)
Released 18 November 1974
Produced by Gus Dudgeon
Recorded at Caribou Ranch, Colorado, USA

PHILADELPHIA FREEDOM/I SAW HER STANDING THERE

(*MCA 40364*)
Released 24 February 1975
Produced by Gus Dudgeon
Recorded at Caribou Ranch, Colorado, USA

SOMEONE SAVED MY LIFE TONIGHT/HOUSE OF CARDS

(*MCA 40421*)
Released 23 June 1975
Produced by Gus Dudgeon
Recorded at Caribou Ranch, Colorado, USA

ISLAND GIRL/SUGAR ON THE FLOOR

(*MCA 40461*)
Released 29 September 1975
Produced by Gus Dudgeon
Recorded at Caribou Ranch, Colorado, USA

I FEEL LIKE A BULLET (IN THE GUN OF ROBERT FORD)/GROW SOME FUNK OF YOUR OWN

(*MCA 40505*)
Released 12 January 1976
Produced by Gus Dudgeon
Recorded at Caribou Ranch, Colorado, USA

DON'T GO BREAKING MY HEART/SNOW QUEEN

(*MCA Rocket 40585*)
Released 21 June 1976
Produced by Gus Dudgeon
Recorded at Eastern Sound, Toronto

SORRY SEEMS TO BE THE HARDEST WORD/SHOULDER HOLSTER

(*MCA/Rocket 40645*)
Released 1 November 1976
Produced by Gus Dudgeon
Recorded at Eastern Sound, Toronto

BITE YOUR LIP (GET UP & DANCE)/CHAMELEON

(*MCA/Rocket 40677*)
Released 31 January 1977
Produced by Gus Dudgeon
Recorded at Eastern Sound, Toronto

EGO/FLINTSTONE BOY

(*MCA 40892*)
Released March 1978
Produced by Elton John/Clive Franks
Recorded at The Mill, Cookham, Surrey

SONG FOR GUY/LOVESICK

(*MCA 40993*)
Released March 1979
Produced by Elton John/Clive Franks
Recorded at The Mill, Cookham, Surrey

MAMA CAN'T BUY YOU LOVE/THREE-WAY LOVE AFFAIR

(*MCA 41042*)
Released June 1979
Produced by Thom Bell
Recorded at Sigma Sound Studios, Philadelphia

MAMA CAN'T BUY YOU LOVE/THREE WAY LOVE AFFAIR/ARE YOU READY FOR LOVE

(*MCA 13921*)
Released June 1979
Produced by Thom Bell
Recorded at Kay Smith Studio, Seattle

VICTIM OF LOVE/STRANGERS

(*MCA 41126*)
Released September 1979
Produced by Pete Bellotte
Recorded at Musicland, Munich

PART-TIME LOVE/I CRY AT NIGHT

(*MCA 40973*)
Released November 1979
Produced by Elton John/Clive Franks
Recorded at The Mill, Cookham, Surrey

JOHNNY B. GOODE/GEORGIA

(*MCA 41159*)
Released December 1979
Produced by Pete Bellotte
Recorded at Musicland, Munich

LITTLE JEANNIE/CONQUER THE SUN

(*MCA 41236*)
Released 17 May 1980
Produced by Elton John/Clive Franks
Recorded at Superbear Studios, Nice

DON'T YA WANNA PLAY THIS GAME NO MORE (SARTORIAL ELOQUENCE)/CARTIER/WHITE MAN DANGER

(*MCA 41293*)
Released August 1980
Produced by Elton John & Clive Franks
Recorded at Superbear Studios, Nice, France

NOBODY WINS/FOOLS IN FASHION

(*Geffen GEF 49722*)
Released May 1981
Produced by Chris Thomas
Recorded at Sunset Sound, Los Angeles

CHLOE

(*Geffen 49788*)
Released July 1981
Produced by Chris Thomas

EMPTY GARDEN

(*Geffen GEF 50049*)
Released March 1982
Produced by Chris Thomas
Recorded at AIR Studios, Monserrat

BLUE EYES

(*Geffen 7-29954*)
Released June 1982
Produced by Chris Thomas
Recorded at AIR Studios, Monserrat

I'M STILL STANDING

(*Geffen 7-29639*)
Released April 1983
Produced by Chris Thomas
Recorded at AIR Studios, Monserrat

KISS THE BRIDE

(*Geffen*)
Released July 1983
Produced by Chris Thomas
Recorded at AIR Studios, Monserrat

I GUESS THAT'S WHY THEY CALL IT THE BLUES

(*Geffen 7-29460*)
Released October 1983
Produced by Chris Thomas
Recorded at AIR Studios, Monserrat

SAD SONGS (SAY SO MUCH)/A SIMPLE MAN

(*Geffen 7-29292*)
Released May 1984
Produced by Chris Thomas
Recorded at AIR Studios, Monserrat

WHO WEARS THESE SHOES?

(*Geffen 7-29189*)
Released August 1984
Produced by Chris Thomas
Recorded at AIR Studios, Monserrat

UK ALBUMS

EMPTY SKY

(*DJM DJLPS 403*)
Released 3 June 1969
Produced by Steve Brown
Recorded at Dick James Studios, London
Side One:
1 **Empty Sky**
2 **Val-Hala**
3 **Western Ford Gateway**
4 **Hymn 2000**
Side Two
5 **Lady What's Tomorrow**
6 **Sails**
7 **The Scaffold**
8 **Skyline Pigeon**
9 **Gulliver-Hay Chewed**
Musicians: Elton, Caleb Quaye, Tony Murray, Roger Pope
Engineer: Frank Owen

ELTON JOHN

(*DJM DJLPS 406*)
Released 10 April 1970
Produced by Gus Dudgeon
Recorded at Trident Studios, London
Side One:
1 **Your Song**
2 **I Need You To Turn To**
3 **Take Me To The Pilot**
4 **No Shoe Strings On Louise**
5 **First Episode At Hienton**
Side Two:
6 **Sixty Years On**
7 **Border Song**
8 **The Greatest Discovery**
9 **The Cage**
10 **The King Must Die**

TUMBLEWEED CONNECTION

(*DJM DJLPS 410*)
Released 30 October 1970
Produced by Gus Dudgeon
Recorded at Trident Studios, London
Side One:
1 **Ballad Of A Well Known Gun**
2 **Come Down In Time**
3 **Country Comfort**
4 **Son Of Your Father**
5 **My Father's Gun**
Side Two:
6 **Where To Now St. Peter**
7 **Love Song**
8 **Amoreena**
9 **Talking Old Soldiers**
10 **Burn Down The Mission**
Musicians: Elton, Caleb Quaye, Roger Pope, Dave Glover, Barry Morgan.
Engineer: Robin G. Cable

17.11.70

(*DJM DJLPS 414*)
Released April 1971
Produced by Gus Dudgeon
Recorded at Dick James Studios, London
Side One:
1 **Take Me To The Pilot**
2 **Honky Tonk Woman**
3 **Sixty Years On**
4 **Can I Put You On**
Side Two:
5 **Bad Side Of The Moon**
6 **Burn Down The Mission**
Musicians: Elton, Nigel Olsson, Dee Murray.
Engineer: Phil Ramone

FRIENDS

(*Paramount SPFL 269*)
Released April 1971
Produced by Gus Dudgeon
Recorded at Trident Studios, London.
Side One:
   1 Friends
   2 Honey Roll
   3 Variations On Friends
   4 Theme (The First Kiss) Seasons
   5 Variations On Michelle's Song
   6 Can I Put You On
Side Two:
   7 Michelle's Song
   8 I Meant To Do My Work Today (A Day In The Country)
   9 XX Four Moods
   10 Seasons Reprise
Musicians: Elton, Nigel Olsson, Dee Murray, Caleb
Quaye, Rex Morris, Paul Buckmaster
Engineer: Robin G. Cable

MADMAN ACROSS THE WATER

(*DJM DJLPH 420*)
Released 5 November 1971
Produced by Gus Dudgeon
Recorded at Trident Studios, London
Side One:
   1 Tiny Dancer
   2 Levon
   3 Razor Face
   4 Madman Across The Water
Side Two:
   5 Indian Sunset
   6 Holiday Inn
   7 Rotten Peaches
   8 All The Nasties
   9 Goodbye
Musicians: Elton, Roger Pope, David Glover, Caleb
Quaye, BJ Cole
Engineer: Robin G. Cable

HONKY CHATEAU

(*DJM DJLPH 423*)
Released 19 May 1972
Produced by Gus Dudgeon
Recorded at Strawberry Studios, Chateau
D'Hierouville, France
Side One:
   1 Honky Cat
   2 Mellow
   3 I Think I'm Gonna Kill Myself
   4 Suzie (Dramas)
   5 Rocket Man (I Think It's Going To Be A Long Long Time)
Side Two:
   6 Salvation
   7 Slave
   8 Amy
   9 Mona Lisas & Mad Hatters
   10 Hercules
Musicians: Elton, Dee Murray, Davey Johnstone, Nigel
Olsson, Jacques Bolognesi
Engineer: Ken Scott

DON'T SHOOT ME I'M ONLY THE PIANO PLAYER

(*DJM DJLPH 427*)
Released 26 January 1973
Produced by Gus Dudgeon
Recorded at Strawberry Studios, Chateau
D'Hierouville, France
Side One:
   1 Daniel
   2 Teacher I Need You
   3 Elderberry Wine
   4 Blues For My Baby And Me
   5 Midnight Creeper
Side Two:
   6 Have Mercy On The Criminal
   7 I'm Gonna Be A Teenage Idol
   8 Texan Love Song
   9 Crocodile Rock
   10 High Flying Bird
Musicians: Elton, Dee Murray, Nigel Olsson, Davey
Johnstone, Ken Scott
Engineer: Ken Scott

GOODBYE YELLOW BRICK ROAD

(DJM DJLPD 1001/2)
Released 5 October 1973
Produced by Gus Dudgeon
Recorded at Strawberry Studios, Chateau
D'Hierouville, France
Side One:
  1 Funeral For A Friend
  2 Love Lies Bleeding
  3 Candle In The Wind
  4 Bennie And The Jets
Side Two:
  5 Goodbye Yellow Brick Road
  6 This Song Has No Title
  7 Grey Seal
  8 Jamaica Jerk Off
  9 I've Seen That Movie Too
Side Three:
10 Sweet Painted Lady
11 The Ballad Of Danny Bailey
12 Dirty Little Girl
13 All The Young Girls Love Alice
Side Four:
14 Your Sister Can't Twist (But She Can Rock &
    Roll)
15 Saturday Night's Alright For Fighting
16 Roy Rogers
17 Social Disease
18 Harmony
Musicians: Elton, Dee Murray, Nigel Olsson, Davey
Johnstone, David Henschel, Leroy Gomez
Engineer: David Henschel

CARIBOU

(DJM DJLPS 439)
Released 28 June 1974
Produced by Gus Dudgeon
Recorded at Caribou Ranch, Colorado, USA
Side One:
  1 The Bitch Is Back
  2 Pinky
  3 Grimsby
  4 Dixie Lily
  5 Solar Prestige A Gammon
  6 You're So Static
Side Two:
  7 I've Seen The Saucers
  8 Stinker
  9 Don't Let The Sun Go Down On Me
10 Ticking
Musicians: Elton, Dee Murray, Nigel Olsson, Davey
Johnstone, Ray Cooper, Dave Henschel
Engineer: Clive Franks

GREATEST HITS

(DJM DJLPH 422)
Released 8 November 1974
Produced by Gus Dudgeon
Recorded at various studios
Side One:
  1 Your Song
  2 Daniel
  3 Honky Cat
  4 Goodbye Yellow Brick Road
  5 Saturday Night's Alright For Fighting
Side Two:
  6 Rocket Man
  7 Candle In The Wind
  8 Don't Let The Sun Go Down On Me
  9 Border Song
10 Crocodile Rock

CAPTAIN FANTASTIC AND THE BROWN DIRT COWBOY

(DJM DJLPX 1)
Released 23 May 1975
Produced by Gus Dudgeon
Recorded at Caribou Ranch, Colorado, USA
Side One:
  1 Captain Fantastic & The Brown Dirt Cowboy
  2 Tower Of Babel
  3 Bitter Fingers
  4 Tell Me When The Whistle Blows
  5 Someone Saved My Life Tonight
Side Two:
  6 (Gotta Get A) Meal Ticket
  7 Better Off Dead
  8 Writing
  9 We All Fall In Love Sometimes
10 Curtains
Musicians: Elton, Dee Murray, Nigel Olsson, Davey
Johnstone, Ray Cooper
Engineer: Jeff Guercio

ROCK OF THE WESTIES

(*DJM DJLPH 464*)
Released 4 October 1975
Produced by Gus Dudgeon
Recorded at Caribou Ranch, Colorado, USA
Side One:
  1 **Medley (Yell Help, Wednesday Night, Ugly)**
  2 **Dan Dare (Pilot Of The Future)**
  3 **Island Girl**
  4 **Grow Some Funk Of Your Own**
  5 **I Feel Like A Bullet (In The Gun Of Robert Ford)**
Side Two:
  6 **Street Kids**
  7 **Hard Luck Story**
  8 **Feed Me**
  9 **Billy Bones And The White Bird**
Musicians: Elton, Kenny Passarelli, Roger Pope, Davey Johnstone, Caleb Quaye
Engineer: Jeff Guercio

HERE AND THERE

(*DJM DJLPH 473*)
Released 30 April 1976
Produced by Gus Dudgeon
Recorded at The Royal Festival Hall, London
Side One:
  1 **Skyline Pigeon**
  2 **Border Song**
  3 **Honky Cat**
  4 **Love Song**
  5 **Crocodile Rock**
Side Two:
  6 **Funeral For A Friend**
  7 **Love Lies Bleeding**
  8 **Rocket Man**
  9 **Benny And The Jets**
10 **Take Me To The Pilot**
Musicians: Elton, Dee Murray, Nigel Olsson, Davey Johnstone, Ray Cooper
Engineers: Phil Dunne, Gus Dudgeon

BLUE MOVES

(*Rocket/EMI ROSP 1*)
Released 22 October 1976
Produced by Gus Dudgeon
Recorded at Eastern Sound, Toronto
Side One:
  1 **Your Starter For. . .**
  2 **Tonight**
  3 **One Horse Town**
  4 **Chameleon**
Side Two:
  5 **Boogie Pilgrim**
  6 **Cage The Songbird**
  7 **Crazy Water**
  8 **Shoulder Holster**
Side Three:
  9 **Sorry Seems To Be The Hardest Word**
10 **Out Of The Blue**
11 **Between Seventeen & Twenty**
12 **The Wide Eyed & Laughing**
13 **Someone's Final Song**
Side Four:
14 **Where's The Shoorah**
15 **If There's A God In Heaven (What's He Waiting For?)**
16 **Idol**
17 **Theme From A Non-Existent TV Series**
18 **Bite Your Lip (Get Up & Dance)**
Musicians: Elton, Kenny Passarelli, Roger Pope, Caleb Quaye, Davey Johnstone
Engineers: Gus Dudgeon/John Stewart

GREATEST HITS VOLUME II

(*DJM DJLPH 20520*)
Released 13 September 1977
Produced by Gus Dudgeon
Recorded at various studios
Side One:
  1 **The Bitch Is Back**
  2 **Lucy In The Sky With Diamonds**
  3 **Sorry Seems To Be The Hardest Word**
  4 **Don't Go Breaking My Heart**
  5 **Someone Saved My Life Tonight**
Side Two:
  6 **Philadelphia Freedom**
  7 **Island Girl**
  8 **Grow Some Funk Of Your Own**
  9 **Benny And The Jets**
10 **Pinball Wizard**

CANDLE IN THE WIND

(*St Michael 2094/0102*)
Released January 1978
Produced by Gus Dudgeon
Recorded at various studios
Side One:
  1 **Skyline Pigeon**
  2 **Take Me To The Pilot**
  3 **Burn Down The Mission**
  4 **Teacher I Need You**
  5 **Rocket Man**
  6 **Don't Let The Sun Go Down On Me**
  7 **Elderberry Wine**
Side Two:
  8 **Bennie And The Jets**
  9 **Midnight Creeper**
  10 **Dan Dare (Pilot Of The Future)**
  11 **Someone Saved My Life Tonight**
  12 **Better Off Dead**
  13 **Grey Seal (original 1970 version)**
  14 **Candle In The Wind**

ELTON JOHN LIVE

(*Pickwick SHM 942*)
Released 1 March 1978
Produced by Gus Dudgeon
Recorded at same studio as *17.11.70*

LONDON AND NEW YORK (LIVE)

(*Pickwick SHM 966*)
Released 1 September 1978
Produced by Gus Dudgeon
Recorded at same studio as *Here and There*

A SINGLE MAN

(*Rocket Train 1*)
Released 16 October 1978
Produced by Elton John/Clive Franks
Recorded at The Mill, Cookham, Berks.
Side One:
  1 **Shine On Through**
  2 **Return To Paradise**
  3 **I Don't Care**
  4 **Big Dipper**
  5 **It Ain't Gonna Be Easy**
Side Two:
  6 **Part-Time Love**
  7 **Georgia**
  8 **Shooting Star**
  9 **Madness**
  10 **Reverie**
  11 **Song For Guy**
Musicians: Elton, Steve Holly, Clive Franks, Ray Cooper, Tim Renwick
Engineers: Phil Dunne, Stuart Epps, Clive Franks

THE ELTON JOHN LIVE COLLECTION

(*Pickwick PDA 047*)
Released 5 February 1979
Produced by Gus Dudgeon
Recorded at same studio as '*17.11.70*'

EARLY YEARS

(*DJM LPS 13833*)
Released 1 August 1979
Produced by Gus Dudgeon except tracks 1, 2 & 3 Steve Brown
Recorded at Dick James Studios, London and Trident Studios, London
Side One:
  1 **Lady Samantha**
  2 **Skyline Pigeon**
  3 **Empty Sky**
  4 **Border Song**
  5 **I Need You To Turn To**
  6 **Sixty Years On**
Side Two:
  7 **Country Comfort**
  8 **Burn Down The Mission**
  9 **Where To Now St Peter**
  10 **Levon**
  11 **Madman Across The Water**
  12 **Friends**

ELTON ROCKS

(*DJM LPS 13834*)
Released 1 August 1979
Produced by Gus Dudgeon
Recorded at various studios
Side One:
1 **Saturday Night's Alright For Fighting**
2 **(Gotta Get A) Meal Ticket**
3 **Screw You**
4 **Teacher I Need You**
5 **Grow Some Funk Of Your Own**
6 **Grey Seal (1973 Version)**
7 **The Bitch Is Back**
Side Two:
8 **Crocodile Rock**
9 **The Cage**
10 **Elderberry Wine**
11 **Whenever You're Ready (We'll Go Steady Again)**
12 **Street Kids**
13 **Midnight Creeper**
14 **Pinball Wizard**

MOODS

(*DJM LPS 13835*)
Released 1 August 1979
Produced by Gus Dudgeon
Recorded at various studios
Side One:
1 **I Feel Like A Bullet (In The Gun Of Robert Ford)**
2 **Mona Lisas & Mad Hatters**
3 **High Flying Bird**
4 **Tiny Dancer**
5 **The Greatest Discovery**
6 **Blues For My Baby & Me**
Side Two:
7 **Harmony**
8 **I've Seen That Movie Too**
9 **Pinky**
10 **It's Me That You Need**
11 **Indian Sunset**
12 **Sweet Painted Lady**
13 **Love Song**

SINGLES

(*DJM LPS 13836*)
Released 1 August 1979
Produced by Gus Dudgeon
Recorded at various studios
Side One:
1 **Your Song**
2 **Rocket Man**
3 **Honky Cat**
4 **Daniel**
5 **Goodbye Yellow Brick Road**
6 **Candle In The Wind**
7 **Don't Let The Sun Go Down On Me**
Side Two:
8 **Lucy In The Sky With Diamonds**
9 **Philadelphia Freedom**
10 **Someone Saved My Life Tonight**
11 **Island Girl**
12 **Bennie And The Jets**

CLASSICS

(*DJM LPS 13837*)
Released 1 August 1979
Produced by Gus Dudgeon
Recorded at various studios
Side One:
1 **Funeral For A Friend**
2 **Love Lies Bleeding**
3 **The Ballad Of Danny Bailey 1909-34**
4 **Ticking**
Side Two:
5 **Texan Love Song**
6 **Captain Fantastic & The Brown Dirt Cowboy**
7 **We All Fall In Love Sometimes**
8 **Curtains**

VICTIM OF LOVE

(*Rocket HSPD 125*)
Released 13 October 1979
Produced by Pete Bellotte
Recorded at Musicland, Munich and Rusk Sound Studios, Hollywood
Side One:
1 **Johnny B. Goode**
2 **Warm Love In A Cold World**
3 **Born Bad**
Side Two:
4 **Thunder In The Night**
5 **Spotlight**
6 **Street Boogie**
7 **Victim Of Love**
Musicians: Keith Forsey, Marcus Miller, Craig Snyder, Tim Cawsfield, Thor Baldursson
Engineer: Peter Liedman

21 AT 33

(*Rocket HSPD 126*)
Released 13 May 1980
Produced by Elton John/Clive Franks
Recorded at Superbear Studios, Nice
Side One:
1 **Chasing The Crown**
2 **Little Jeannie**
3 **Sartorial Eloquence**
4 **Two Rooms At The End Of The World**
Side Two:
5 **White Lady White Powder**
6 **Dear God**
7 **Never Gonna Fall In Love Again**
8 **Take Me Back**
9 **Give Me The Love**
Musicians: Elton, Nigel Olsson, James Newton-Howard,
Ritchie Zito, J. Horn
Engineers: Patrick Jaunead, Clive Franks

LADY SAMANTHA

(*DJM 22085*)
Released 13 October 1980
Recorded at various studios
Side One:
1 **Rock & Roll Madonna**
2 **Whenever You're Ready (We'll Go Steady Again)**
3 **Bad Side Of The Moon**
4 **Jack Rabbit**
5 **Into The Old Man's Shoes**
6 **It's Me That You Need**
7 **Ho! Ho! Ho! Who'd Be A Turkey At Christmas?**
   Side Two:
8 **Skyline Pigeon**
9 **Screw You**
10 **Just Like Strange Rain**
11 **Grey Seal**
12 **The Honey Roll**
13 **Lady Samantha**
14 **Friends**

THE VERY BEST OF ELTON JOHN

(*K-TEL NE 1094*)
Released 13 October 1980
Produced by Gus Dudgeon
Recorded at various studios
Side One:
1 **Your Song**
2 **Goodbye Yellow Brick Road**
3 **Daniel**
4 **Song For Guy**
5 **Candle In The Wind**
6 **Friends**
7 **Tiny Dancer**
8 **Rocket Man (I Think It's Gonna Be A Long Long Time)**
Side Two:
9 **Don't Go Breaking My Heart**
10 **Sorry Seems To Be The Hardest Word**
11 **Border Song**
12 **Someone Saved My Life Tonight**
13 **Mona Lisas & Mad Hatters**
14 **Harmony**
15 **High Flying Bird**
16 **Don't Let The Sun Go Down On Me**

MILESTONES (1970-1980 A DECADE OF GOLD)

(*K-TEL TU 2640*)
Released November 1980
Produced by Gus Dudgeon
Recorded at various studios
Side One:
1 **Don't Go Breaking My Heart**
2 **Island Girl**
3 **The Bitch Is Back**
4 **Honky Cat**
5 **Bennie & The Jets**
6 **Someone Saved My Life Tonight**
7 **Don't Let The Sun Go Down On Me**
8 **Sorry Seems To Be The Hardest Word**
Side Two:
9 **Mama Can't Buy You Love**
10 **Philadelphia Freedom**
11 **Crocodile Rock**
12 **Rocket Man**
13 **Daniel**
14 **Lucy In The Sky With Diamonds**
15 **Your Song**
16 **Goodbye Yellow Brick Road**

THE FOX

(*Rocket Train 16*)
Released 20 May 1981
Produced by Chris Thomas
Recorded at Sunset Sound, Davlen Studios, Village
Recorders, Los Angeles, USA and Superbear, Nice,
France and EMI, Abbey Road, London
Side One:
  1 **Breaking Down The Barriers**
  2 **Heart In The Right Place**
  3 **Just Like Belgium**
  4 **Nobody Wins**
  5 **Fascist Faces**
Side Two:
  6 **Carla**
  7 **Heels Of The Wind**
  8 **Elton's Song**
  9 **The Fox**
Musicians: Elton, Nigel Olsson, Dee Murray, Ritchie
Zito, Jim Horn

JUMP UP

(*Rocket HISPD 23*)
Released 1982
Produced by Chris Thomas
Recorded at Air Studios, Monserratt
Side One:
  1 **Dear John**
  2 **Spiteful Child**
  3 **Ball And Chain**
  4 **Legal Boys**
  5 **I Am Your Robot**
  6 **Blue Eyes**
Side Two:
  7 **Empty Garden**
  8 **Princess**
  9 **Where Have All The Good Times Gone?**
  10 **All Quiet On The Western Front**
Musicians: Elton, Davey Johnstone, Dee Murray, Nigel
Olsson

TOO LOW FOR ZERO

(*Rocket HISPD 24*)
Released 1983
Recorded at Air Studios, Monserrat
Produced by Chris Thomas
Side One:
  1 **Cold As Christmas**
  2 **I'm Still Standing**
  3 **Too Low For Zero**
  4 **Religion**
  5 **I Guess That's Why They Call It The Blues**
Side Two:
  6 **Crystal**
  7 **Kiss The Bride**
  8 **Whipping Boy**
  9 **Saint**
  10 **One More Arrow**
Musicians: Elton, Davey Johnstone, Dee Murray, Nigel
Olsson.

BREAKING HEARTS

(*Rocket HISPD 25 (UK)/Geffen GHS 24031 (US)*)
Released June 1984
Producer Chris Thomas
Recorded at AIR Studios, Monserrat
Side One:
  1 **Restless**
  2 **Slow Down George (She's Poison)**
  3 **Who Wears These Shoes?**
  4 **Breaking Hearts (Ain't What It Used To Be)**
  5 **Li'l 'Fridgerator**
Side Two
  1 **Passengers**
  2 **In Neon**
  3 **Burning Buildings**
  4 **Did He Shoot Her?**
  5 **Sad Songs (Say So Much)**